FAILURE AIN'T FINAL

BRIAN ANDERSON-PAYNE

ISBN: 978-0-9835083-3-5

PUBLISHED BY:

TBAPP Publishing, LLC
P. O. Box 33864
Decatur, GA 30033-0864
thebapproject@yahoo.com
Please visit our website at
www.failureaintfinal.com
or www.briananersonpayne.com.
Online ordering is available for all products.

DEDICATION

I have a quote that says, *"It's quite difficult to know who really loves until you've exposed a reason NOT to!"* If *anyone* has been given a reason to *run away*, it's my wife, Ruby. I dedicate this book to you because of your dedication to your God, yourself, then to me. Many people quote scripture, but you work to live it!

YOU are the realest!

CONTENTS

Acknowledgments

My Editor, **Bethany Sledge** – I always feel safe in your hands! **Marcus McCurry** (Cover design & Book Layout – You went over and beyond the call of duty on this project! Thanks Bro! **Michelle Parker Wetnight** (Back cover photo) Your work *still* speaks volumes! **Bishop Jim Swilley** – My life is better because of you, Bro! **Gwendolyn McCalep** – You're much more than a all-in, dedicated assistant to me, you're family! My Mom (**Neoma Smith**) & my daughter (**Victorious Dior Anderson-Payne**) – You two ladies don't have to do any more than breathe for acknowledgement! ☺ To my dear family, friends & supporters who stood by me through the darkest seasons of the birthing process, please receive this book as evidence that "Failure Ain't Final!" As you have done me, I now write to *love you to life!*

–Brian Anderson-Payne

The gospel is good news. Period.

In *Failure Ain't Final!*, Brian Anderson-Payne taps directly into the essence of the gospel, which is simply that good news given for and available to–everyone.

This brave new book is Bishop Payne's personal labor of love and is, in fact, full of nothing but good news . . . good news that goes right to the heart of every individual, good news that is truly relevant and universally understood. This volume is *relevant* because every person, without exception, faces failure at one time or another; it is also *understood* because everyone who has experienced it must decide if, in the big picture, the failure will make or break him or her.

Proverbs 24:16 says that even if a righteous person falls seven times (and seven, by the way, is the number for infinity), that one has the ability to get up again. *Failure Ain't Final!* is a challenge to those who have fallen, to believe that they can rise once more . . . a shot of spiritual adrenaline in the arm . . . a confirmation that there is a light at the end of the tunnel . . . a reminder that the gifts and callings of God are, indeed, irrevocable . . . a positive affirmation that simply says, "Yes, you can!"

Failure Ain't Final! is a book that is based on more than just a concept or an ideal. It is the result of truths learned in the laboratory of life. The author writes with authority because he shares from a place of experience. This is his own message . . . a message of hope, tried in the fire, from a survivor and a champion who knows of what he speaks.

If you have fallen and think you can't get up, stop wasting your time on the floor of self-pity and/or self-condemnation and read the book. Read it and get started on your road to recovery and restoration. You really can do it. If you've just been waiting for someone to come along to convince you of that, this is the good news you have been waiting for!

—Bishop Jim Swilley
Church in the Now
Now Ministries

Introduction

Thursday, December 3, 2009, I turned on my computer and began typing. I thought I was writing a book called *Doo-Doo on My Gators*. Soon after, I changed the title to *Did He Just Say, "Oops"?* However, that didn't really grab me either. Saturday, December 5, I decided the title would be *Failure Isn't Final*, but vacillating, as I often do, I changed my mind again, Monday, December 7, and named the book *How to Fail Successfully!* As the evidence in your hand shows, I changed my mind again. Well, the title isn't nearly as important as the product, and now you have both.

> *Most great people have attained their greatest success just one step beyond their greatest failure.*
> *– Napoleon Hill, Personal Success author*

I'll begin by saying something that may cause you to question what you have gotten yourself into by purchasing this book. Brace yourself. Here it goes: *God needs you to fail.* Hello? Are you still there? Are you still reading? Great! If you are waiting for a retraction, I'm not going to take the phrase back. I meant every word. God needs you to fail. I can pretty much guarantee that the scope of your perspective will change when you do.

Fall seven times, stand up eight.
— *Japanese proverb*

Now, hold on a second. Before you throw up your hands in celebration and start searching for the biggest no-no you can possibly find, you need to read more first. As a matter of fact, if that's the reaction you had, that statement may not apply to you. After all, remember: Romans 6:1-2 (*The Message*) asks the question: *So what do we do? Keep on sinning so God can keep on forgiving? I should hope not!*

Failure is the place where God proves you didn't earn His love anyway!
— *Brian Anderson-Payne*

In all sincerity, I am not suggesting that any of us should look for an opportunity to fail, mess up, or blow it in any way. And if someone tells you that you should, grab your coat and run for the border. No one who really sets out to serve God with all his heart, soul, and mind even desires to fail! I will go a step further to say the person who exalts failure probably won't purchase this book anyway. However, while we may not seek to fail, failure will be one of the most powerful assets you have. For you who have been suffocating in the chamber of guilt, crumbling under the burden of shame, or dying while tied to the shackle of un-forgiveness, I offer the wisdom of this book as a lifeguard offering a life preserver to the waterlogged victim.

I'm quite sure I startled you with the statement, "God needs you to fail." Now, allow me to explain why: **You are one good failure away from being used by God!**

Researching information for this book had me looking through all kinds of writings about different subjects. I was inundated with facts about success. I understand why, too. Everybody wants to be successful, right? No one ever starts out as a child and thinks, *When I grow up, I want to be a great big failure!* Certainly not. All types of writings exist to teach you how to be successful in business, in family, in finances, and the list goes on and on and on.

> *Living then, as every one of you does, in pure grace, it's important that you not misinterpret yourselves as people who are bringing this goodness to God. No, God brings it all to you. The only accurate way to under-stand ourselves is by what God is and by what he does for us, not by what we are and what we do for him.*
>
> — *Romans 12:3 (Message)*

What I noticed was, as there is a great deal of information about success, there isn't as much about failure. Why aren't more people writing about failure? Does the mention of the word bring a "downer" feeling? Is it possible even to consider the word "success" without the concept of the word "failure" lingering somewhere near? Interestingly, several of the success stories encourage you to see failure as part of the journey to success, but not nearly enough time has been spent on the subject.

I believe failure is the place where the success journey begins. Success is attached to failure just as rain is attached to sunshine, like cold is attached to heat, like darkness is attached to light. One doesn't gain its identity from the other, but it sure helps provide greater clarity, doesn't it?

While the word "failure" is mentioned often throughout this book, that is to give us a clear understanding of what failure is so you can recognize what it's not. One of the things you are sure to discover that it is not, is final!

I want you to give great consideration to three parts or sections, as they are the environments or mind-sets I address throughout this book. Each should be considered carefully as we handle each other. I have identified the sections from a verse of Scripture we will use often, Galatians 6:1. The parts or sections are pre-failure, acknowledged failure, and post-failure.

Part One – Pre-failure

Brothers, if someone is caught in a sin, you who are spiritual should restore him gently. But watch yourself, or you also may be tempted.

–Galatians 6:1

This text is written in several versions. There are small variations, but for the most part, the text versions are consistent. In the New International Version I have used, the sentence begins with the word "brothers." This is an extremely significant classification to precede the following instructions. It informs us of what group of people is being addressed.

So far in the text, we have no idea of what is or is not about to happen. All we have is an address or identification. By definition, brothers and sisters are individuals who have at least one parent in common. In the figurative religious sense, which we are using, each of us is connected through our Father, God. The word here informs us of the fact that the listeners should have a sense of camaraderie, unity, or connectedness. This bears great importance because of the implication that family will carry a greater concern for each other than unrelated persons would. Because of the fallen state of mankind, I'm sure that someone reading this would beg to differ with my depiction of family. Certainly, some families, unfortunately, display great acts of disloyalty and betrayal. However, we are speaking of the ideal or God's intended sense of family. In design, family would be the unit to display the greatest sense and example of love imaginable. Therefore, the implication in the text is that a group of individuals who view each other as close family is being addressed. A sense of protection for each other would be necessary before expressing the words that follow. This is important to you and me because without these clarifications, we could find ourselves expecting certain protection or restoration to come from individuals who have not the slightest desire to give it. It is a sad truth, but not every living being has a concern for the well-being of other living beings.

This leads to the second implication of the word "brothers" in the text. In order to be considered a brother or sister by the early church was not as simple a task as it seems to be in many Christian churches today. Christianity was not the popular religion of the day, so it was sometimes dangerous to be considered a follower of Christ. It wasn't the kind of thing a person would do just because someone else in his family did it. Unlike today, they didn't just throw the title "Christian" around lightly. Therefore, if he was one, he meant to be one!

Christians were often challenged to display their true concern for others as the believers did in the Book of Acts by bringing their personal property together to sell it for the well-being of other believers (Acts 2:45). Or often they would place themselves in danger by protecting other Christians who were in a far more dangerous situation at the time (Acts 23:16-22).

Basically, if one was a Christian, he truly knew he was, and so did others. The goal was to please God by demonstrating obedience to the words of Christ and love for self and the fellow brothers and sisters in Christ.

Unfortunately, even within the walls of the twenty-first-century church, we don't always see biblical love and support going forth. I believe this is caused by one of two reasons. One is because Christianity is extremely popular today, and many people seemingly ascribe to the Christian faith without truly committing to take on the Christian principles and practices. In short, there are many who bear the name "Christian" who chooses not to take up honestly or commit to the practices of Christ.

The second reason we don't always see biblical love going forth is because of a lack of accurate teaching that defines biblical love truly. More often, many hear instructions of love within our comfort zones or within our personal abilities to achieve easily. However, biblical love is much greater than any individual. It will take us outside our comfort zones and will push us far beyond anything we are capable of achieving by or of ourselves. We are only capable of biblical love as we allow God to love individuals through us. This will sometimes compel us to love individuals at times when we don't understand why we are doing so. It will sometimes not even make sense to our logic. This is because we are no longer in charge, and now God loves someone through our hearts and bodies.

Ground Zero

From Paul's word, "brothers," even before he has addressed the issue, we already know that the atmosphere is one of love, consideration, godly obedience, and support. Believers should live lives that display an earnest and honest effort to honor the instruction of Christ on a daily basis. This isn't solely or mainly to please others but in obedience to the words of Christ. In other words, we don't do it to gain God's approval. We do it because we have God's approval. No doubt, there will be places where we miss the mark, but this should not be a common dilemma. Remember, to "restore" means to put something back in its proper position or status. If we haven't come into the knowledge or desire of living our most obedient life, it will be difficult to determine a position to be restored to!

Pre-failure, notice an environment of support (not condemnation or judgment) of other believers that consistently lends itself to one's development as a person of faith. Surround yourself with people who sincerely want to be the best they can be. People who are honest with God and themselves will have a different temperament with you than those who aren't. They understand how much work it takes to keep oneself in check. Therefore, while they may have an understandably high standard, they should be less likely to place an unrealistic expectation on others. As a rule of thumb, I believe it is unfair to set an expectation on others that you will not place on yourself. All of us should desire to live our most effective lives.

I titled this section, "Ground Zero," because it's the

starting place. While it may not have been everyone's reality, I'm sure we all understand what a difference it would have made to live or interact in such an environment of encouragement, accountability, and love.

Part Two — Acknowledged Failure

Things get a little tricky here. I titled this section, "Acknowledged Failure," because we are focusing on something specific. I believe we have failures continuously throughout our day. At times it's a mean thought we have as we drive home in after work traffic. Sometimes we pass a street beggar, and due to the hustle and bustle of our day, we never take the time to acknowledge his request for coins though we have ample.

> *Brothers, if someone is caught in a sin, you who are spiritual should restore him gently. But watch yourself, or you also may be tempted.*
> *—Galatians 6:1*

We have "small" failures (at the risk of erroneously placing degrees on failures) all the time. These things are included in our daily repenting prayers. However, we are not speaking of these. We are speaking of those failures that have the ability to get into our psyche and begin to hold us captive. I know that because of the language Paul used.

Notice the words, "If someone is caught in a sin." The word for "caught" means literally to be "detected, overtaken, surprised." One commentary explains the term: "Because this word appears in the passive voice in this context, it may connote the idea of surprise: someone suddenly entrapped or discovered in an unseemly situation or heinous act."[1] While we who are mature understand that there can be no truth to the statement, "The devil made me do it," there is truth to the statement that you can unwisely find yourself in situations you did not expect or plan to be in. There is no limit to the traps and snares you may discover if left unguarded. These pitfalls can be confusing because, ultimately, every move we make is a choice. If you spoke unkind words to someone, while it feels comforting to defend your actions, you really didn't lose control over your mouth. If you had an affair, you didn't just wake up in a strange bed. No, even those steps were decisions you made. Yet it is possible to allow yourself to be enticed to the degree that wrong starts to look right . . . until you have committed the act and reality sets in. Once that happens, even something you willfully chose to do becomes quite burdensome to you. The situation becomes really confusing to unbelievers because all they see is the act. They fail to see how the believer feels about his sin. After making dumb decisions and receiving questions, "How could you do something so stupid?" I have had to admit I was the first to ask that question! Not everyone realizes that

---

[1] George, T. (2001). *Vol. 30: Galatians* (electronic ed.) Logos Library System; The New American Commentary (409). Nashville: Broadman & Holman Publishers.

it's possible to do something when you can't figure out why you did it! It's like seeing a pig and a sheep stuck in mud. Both animals are in the same mud, but they don't feel the same way. The pig loves it. The sheep cries in agony.

When I hear the word "caught," I think of a chase taking place. Remember playing chase, commencing with the words, "Catch me if you can"? The objective of the game was to avoid being caught. Therefore, you gave escape your best effort. You didn't sit restfully on the side of the field, waiting to be caught. The same is true in the scenarios of life. Decent people don't expect to be tied up in failures, sins, and so on. No. You give it your best shot daily to avoid these things. I know that some people will try to make it seem like a simple task, but that's probably because they're looking at someone else's struggle. The reality is, there are things that all of us have to work at avoiding. Some things cause little to no problem to avoid or resist. Other things you simply have to run from! Unfortunately, there are times or situations when we don't run fast enough. When that is the case, we are caught by sin! I don't have to describe the difference between someone being caught and someone lying down. If you've been caught, you, better than anyone else, know it. It's not the rewarding feeling that would be expected. What flesh said would be rewarding actually feels like a burden.

The idea of being "caught" goes further than being

caught by others. Sometimes you are caught by yourself. The personal conviction of a failure (moral or otherwise) is tremendously more difficult to conquer than the conviction that others bring. You can get away from people much easier than you can get away from yourself. Wherever you go, there you are! I believe this is why the rest of the Galatians verse is recorded. Overcoming personal perceptions about your own failures is so difficult that God enlists others to help to do it. Restoration is not a one-man or one-woman show.

Part Three – Post-failure

After the failure has been identified and addressed, a whole new procedure begins. Restoration! Now, all the king's horses and all the king's men begin the process of putting Humpty-Dumpty together again! We will discuss that in great detail in later chapters.

How do you fix broken pieces? Better yet, how do you fix broken people? Some folks would step back and say, "It's a job for God." True! It certainly is. But guess what? God is only going to do it through you and me! So the steps and direction of restoration lie in the hands of God alone, but responsibility and the process of restoration lie in your hands and mine.

With that being said, let's identify the parts of the whole: God, the broken party, and the restorers. Each has a significant part to play. This book focuses mostly on the instructions or "how-to" for the latter two.

While I have stated a truth that restoration isn't a one person party, one person certainly has a substantial role to play – **you!** This writing assumes that you've come to the place where you want to be restored. I often say, "God helps those who help themselves, and He also helps those who just don't know what to do!" That is true. How He helps those who don't know what to do does not always mean He does it for them. Sometimes, He sustains them until they can make decisions for themselves on a direction.

Defeating the Enemy "In-a-Me"!

If situations and circumstances have knocked you down, you have to decide to get up! You have to choose to move forward. While it may be extremely difficult for some, it still has to be done. The greatest obstacle to your moving forward won't be your naysayers. It won't even be the mistake you made. Contrary to popular belief, it won't be the devil. But it will be an enemy. You see, my greatest obstacle is the enemy "in-a-me"!

The things from without are not what causes the greatest trouble. It's the thing within! External forces have considerably less power when they lack internal support. Think about it. Someone telling you what you cannot accomplish only matters if you believe him. Therefore, your first assignment is overcoming the debilitating thoughts that you tell yourself. First, you have to believe that you are not what you did and that the story is not over for you!

What you say to yourself matters more than anything! Even God teaches us this point. If you believe you can't survive, you can't. If you believe this is just the beginning, it is. If you believe that touching the hem of His garment will make you whole, it will. Remember, what you say to yourself matters, so say what God says! What He says is that He came to give you an abundant life, so don't sit there and die!

Right Focus

Watch what you focus on. See the whole picture of yourself and not just the image you arrived at after making a mistake. Don't focus on the misstep. Focus on the big picture, the you who God designed you to be. Remember, you are not what you did! I think it can be best described with an article I read online. The author is unknown, but the writing is powerful.

> Both the hummingbird and the vulture fly over the nation's deserts.
> All vultures see is rotting meat, because that is what they look for. They thrive on that diet. But hummingbirds ignore the smelly flesh of dead animals. Instead, they look for the colorful blossoms of desert plants.
> The vultures live on what was. They live on the

past. They fill themselves with what is dead and gone. But hummingbirds live on what is. They seek new life. They fill themselves with freshness and live. Each bird finds what it is looking for. We all do.

See what God sees, say what God says, and let the restoration process begin!

The Spiritual Ones

While it seems a wonderful assignment to restore someone, not everyone is entrusted with the assignment. According to Galatians, only the "spiritual" ones are employed, only those who have a developed relationship with God. This doesn't mean they are better than others, but they are certainly more mature. They can be trusted with the failure of another. They won't be guilty of over-criticizing one's failure. Neither will they sweep it under the carpet as if it doesn't matter. They'll discern the time for a strong talk and the time for loving encouragement. One size does not fit all. Different stages require different approaches.

Some individuals have learned how to give a word in "due season." There is a right response and a right time for it. Sometimes you can have a right word, but a right word given at a wrong time can be disastrous. Restoration greatly demands one who can know the right timing. The spiritual ones operate restoration not from an angle of false piety. They operate from the angle of self-consideration. They, as the Bible says, "consider themselves." You will always receive different treatment from someone who places himself in your shoes. When we can place ourselves in another's shoes, we can fairly consider the treatment we would wish to receive. An environment of individuals pre-pared to serve others with extreme consideration they would wish to receive is an atmosphere prepared for restoration.

THE END

Every new beginning comes from some other beginning's end.

–Seneca

1
ON YOUR MARK, SET, FAIL!

No one ever plans to fail! I'm just putting it out there. You've never asked a kid what he or she wants to be when that one grows up and received the answer, "A great big failure." Be honest. It has never happened, has it? It just doesn't happen that way. Because if it did, I'm sure we would have seen it on reality television by now!

Typically, the very word "failure" creates a negative overtone. I'm not suggesting we should create a special holiday for the word. Then again, maybe I am. Maybe we should have "Failures Day." Why? Well, just think of it. Most of us have never heard success stories celebrated in the absence of failure. More often than not, the conversation of those who have succeeded surrounds what seems to be confident acknowledgment of the many failures they have had.

You don't really have to be a sports advocate to be aware of the many failures in the early career of Michael Jordan, who is one of today's most celebrated athletic figures. Henry Ford went broke five times before founding the successful Ford Motor Company. R. H. Macy started seven businesses that failed before he finally hit big with his store in New York City. Harland David Sanders, perhaps better known as Colonel Sanders of Kentucky Fried Chicken, had his secret chicken recipe rejected 1,009 times before a restaurant accepted it. The multimillionaire Walt Disney was fired by a newspaper editor because "he lacked imagination and had no good ideas." Bill Gates and Oprah Winfrey are a few more of our world's most successful failures.

Failure isn't an identity—it's an experience. It doesn't define who you are; it identifies what you've experienced.
–Brian Anderson-Payne

What I find interesting is the number of times we acknowledge a person's success while that one views the success in light of the failure he or she has experienced. Success is all the more satisfying when you are aware of the failures you had to overcome to reach it! For many, it's hard to conceive that anyone would ever tell Oprah Winfrey she was "unfit" for television. What? The big O? That might be impossible for some of us even to imagine. Well, it might be impossible today, but recall that we are catching the end of the movie. We weren't around to witness those awful days that held, I imagine, unbearable depression, questions, and doubt. However, those uncomfortable events simply sparked something in her that forced her to decide to succeed in spite of failure.

Isn't it a wonderful aspect of life when you are able to get beyond crushing experiences that seem to snatch the life out of you, move on, and still excitedly reach your goals? Experiences like those make it difficult for others to imagine your past was as bad as you know it was. That is what will happen for many of you reading this book. I know it certainly is what happened (and continues to happen) for me. The proof is in the pudding! That's why this book exists.

You see, God is all about bringing success stories out of failures. We know that, we have heard that, we are excited when others say that, but somehow, when we have those experiences that cause us to feel unable to get up again or recover, we sometimes forget that.

Many of us have suffered through things we never dreamed we would experience: failed marriages; loss of dreams, hopes, and visions; ministry collapses; careers gone awry; scandal, hurt, and betrayal; and the list could go on and on. The difficult reality to swallow is that God was not surprised by what you went through. How could He have been? He is the all-knowing God, right? So there never is a moment when He doesn't possess all information past, present, and future. "Learning" isn't one of His better qualities because "learning" means there is something He didn't already know (that includes your entire past and all mistakes). I'll even suggest that your failure is part of the big picture of His plan for your life. You see, many of us felt we knew God pretty well. Perhaps, we did. But I can guarantee we didn't know Him nearly as well as we did after certain experiences.

That is exactly why He allows certain experiences to transpire. Things we would not touch with a ten-foot pole are simply tools of effectiveness in the hands of an all-knowing, wise God. Think about it! God took Satan and manipulated him to accost Job just to confirm that not everyone serving God does so because of the blessings God provides for him (Job 1). Or look how God belittled and embarrassed Egypt's pharaoh to have His own name exalted by His people. That was simply genius! But we would never have tried that. Most of us wouldn't dare temporarily place our lovely but rebellious daughter in the home of an abuser so she could come to appreciate how well she has it under our roof! But God did.

> *For by now I could have stretched out my hand and struck you and your people with a plague that would have wiped you off the earth. But I have raised you up for this very purpose, that I might show you my power and that my name might be proclaimed in all the earth.*
>
> *—Exodus 9:15-16*

All through Scripture, we can see God setting the stage to present Himself to His people in ways that they never knew Him before. When God was ready to introduce Himself as Abraham's provider, He allowed Abraham to experience lack on Mount Moriah (Genesis 22). When God was ready to introduce Himself to Israel as their healer, He allowed them to undergo a sickness from snake bites (Numbers 21). Now, I'm not saying that God sent your particular situation to you. Many times, a situation is a direct blessing, result, or consequence of our own choices. But I am saying it was obviously on the menu before you arrived, and it's going to be the very thing that propels you into your greatness!

I can just hear thoughts now: *Are you suggesting that God sent. . . ?* It's impossible for some even to imagine God in that way because they are thinking of someone else's situation and making a bad judgment call. I am suggesting that God knows exactly what it takes for each of us to become the person He desires us to be. The Lord knows exactly what situations, circumstances, and environments are needed for us to be most productive. Those necessary requirements are different for each of us.

Watch this. Moses murdered a man secretly and ran away. Did God tell him to murder that guy? No. Years later, however, whose passion for Israel did God use to receive glory? Yep, you guessed it—Mr. Murderer, Moses.

Whatever failure you've committed is indeed real. I am not saying it's no big deal. If it is sin or a weight, it is a big deal! Yet I want you to know that God isn't intimidated by any failure you have had or will have, and He wants to take that failure and turn it around to produce His glory in your life, if you'll let Him.

What's Your Big Deal?

I'm always amazed when I turn on the television or computer and hear people talking about God using your failures for His glory and then explain it with some issue like, "You didn't pay your tithe last week." I'm not making light of not paying tithes. In my house, tithing is a big deal for us not to avoid a curse but rather to receive a blessing. But when you're a leader who has dealt with things like adulterous affairs or children born out of wedlock, you kind of look to hear things with a little more dirt on them, if you know what I mean.

Please understand: I know sin is sin, and there is no big sin or little sin in God's eyes. However, certainly there are different degrees of sin in people's eyes. And sometimes, other people's opinion can have great impact on how we view ourselves, initially anyway. So we who have committed the "big" sins look for someone to open the Scriptures and to give us encouragement from the heart of God as well.

I remember ripping the covers off books, trying to hear someone say, "Yes, you've done this horrible thing. There will be uncomfortable fruit from your actions. God isn't happy with what you've done, yet He still loves you! Nothing has changed about that." It seemed people preached the forgiveness of God to the point one became a churchgoing believer. From there, the message somehow changed from forgiveness to one's personal responsibility. So from what I often heard, one was either someone who had no relationship with God and could receive His unconditional love, or one was a believer who should have known better and now has to pay the piper. I'm not so sure that's the image God wanted us to have concerning who He is and how His love works.

What It Should Really Look Like

Here is the message we have heard from Christ and now announce to you: God is light, and in him there is no darkness at all. So if we

say we have fellowship with God, but we continue living in darkness, we are liars and do not follow the truth. But if we live in the light, as God is in the light, we can share fellowship with each other. Then the blood of Jesus, God's Son, cleanses us from every sin. If we say we have no sin, we are fooling ourselves, and the truth is not in us.
—I John 1:58 (New Century Version)

The true God message is armed with both responsibility and forgiveness. It's undeniable that we have a responsibility to follow God and to become more and more like Him each day. Every true believer desires to be more like Christ. People may often look at your failures and conclude you're just a heathen. But you know the honest truth. Is your desire and trajectory to be like Christ? In light of your weakness, struggles, and fleshly desires, is your uttermost, heartfelt aspiration to be like Jesus? The writer of Psalm 42 said (NRSV): **As a deer longs for flowing streams, so my soul longs for you, O God. My soul thirsts for God, for the living God.**

The image here is of an animal that needs water for sustained life. The animal needs water every day. This is not a need that only appears after a long run through the woods. The believer needs God daily, not just in seasons of trouble. The need certainly might be increased during those difficult times, but it always exists.

I get that! I have had times when my actions looked nothing like God, yet my hunger was always for

Him even if it didn't look that way. This may sound strange to some, but it will make total sense to others. It is possible to act in ways that directly contradict God's instructions, yet simultaneously despise the fact that you're where you are. You can go across the street, walk on your own feet, get there, and hate the fact that you even wanted to be there. (Don't worry; we will discuss that in depth later.)

In our pursuit of God, we will have times when we miss the mark. Sometimes we miss it *big!* Contrary to popular bulldog messages, the size of your failure does not back up or scare God. Typically, it only causes that reaction in religious people. The only thing you could do to back God up is reject faith in the work of Calvary. Even then, you wouldn't back God up; you back away. Actually, God is drawn to one who blows it and knows it . . . when blowing it is linked to a sincere cry for His love, comfort, forgiveness, restoration, and guidance.

> *The Son of man came to find lost people and save them.*
> *—Luke 19:10 (New Century Version)*

> *He has not punished us as our sins should be punished; he has not repaid us for the evil we have done. As high as the sky is above the earth, so great is his love for those who respect him. He has taken our sins away from us as far as the east is from west. The LORD has mercy on those who respect him, as a father has mercy on his children. He knows*

*how we were made; he remembers that we
are dust.*
— *Psalm 103:10-14 (New Century Version)*

Here's the deal. In order to fulfill His purpose, Christ needs those who need Him. He came to lead, guide, and direct those who would acknowledge and admit they are lost. It's amazing how many people seem to think that the merciful side of God is a one-shot deal. The assumption is once Christ comes into your life, you're no longer sick, you are no longer lost, and you will never again be in trouble. That's just not true. That's why the Holy Spirit still dwells here. Yes, we are born again, but who knows a brand new baby who came from the womb, got in the car, and drove himself home? He is brand new. He has to learn how to navigate life in this new place.

Indeed, once Christ's Spirit comes into my life, I'm positioned in a place where I'll never be without Him again. However, I still have to grow and develop into the person I was designed to be. That is no instant, overnight ordeal. It takes a minute. It takes trial and error. It takes growing, learning, and developing. It takes failing!

So failures aren't deal breakers with God. He read the "car facts" before He purchased the car. He knew there were kinks, bruises, nicks, and dings. He isn't intimidated by them, either. He signed up for the long haul.

Failures Work Better

The reality is most of the encouraging characters of Scripture encourage us because of what God used them in spite of. Here's a fact: Every effective person in Scripture failed (at some point) but Christ.

We'll discuss each of them later, but countless individuals have found encouragement from the steps, missteps, and redirection of people like Peter, Paul, David, and Moses.

What could be worse than denying knowing Christ? Have you ever experienced the guilty feelings that come from publicly behaving in such a way that suggests you have no clue of who Christ is? God forbid those missteps be seen by others who don't profess a faith in Christ. Sometimes situations like those cause us to feel totally unworthy of proclaiming believer status. It can make you feel like you should just throw in the "Christ towel" and conclude you're not worthy of Him. That's what Peter felt like when three times he denied even knowing Jesus! Now, I have to be honest. I would be totally offended by one of my closest friends leaving me in a jam by myself and denying knowing me. I mean, the whole scope of friendship is based on one being there in difficult times as well as pleasant times, right? We often determine our true friends based on those who are willing to stand with us even in the most difficult seasons of our lives. We often consider those who leave us "associates" or "friendly enemies."

However, Christ went beyond the offense of Peter's denial, and after His resurrection, He tenderly addressed Peter and restored him to his assignment.

Why was He so forgiving there? Why didn't He use that to stop Peter's ever being on His team again? Because He understands that failure isn't final! He understood that while Peter had blown it big time, he wouldn't always blow it like that. Peter's unfortunate experience became an empowering agent for the rest of his life. So it is with me, and so it is with you. No matter how many times you have messed up in certain areas, for the truly sincere, God leaves an opportunity to express His endless mercy and restoration power.

An extremely important part of the journey is realizing a total dependence on God. That sounds like a cliché, but it is quite easy to convince oneself you are depending on God when, in reality, you're doing nothing of the sort. What does it mean to depend on God? *Depend* means "to place reliance or trust" (Webster). Therefore, our dependence on God is linked to our trust in Him. You won't trust in a person with whom you don't have a relationship. And you won't have real relationship with a person you don't share experiences with. Therefore, our experiences develop relationship, which enables us to trust.

You might be wondering why I named this chapter, "On Your Mark, Set, Fail!" Let me explain. Most of us are familiar and comfortable with the three-command start. There are several: "On your mark, set, go!"

"Ready, aim, fire!" "Lights, camera, action!" There are more, but I think you get the point.

The three-command call is the one we have come to know and to expect before a race. "On your mark" means it's time to get in your lane. No more lollygagging. Get your mind off the previous conversations or the things you were previously dealing with. "Get set" means to set your body in position for what's about to happen. Set your mind right. "Go" means simply that. Take off! Now, those steps have to be in order. If you skip the first two steps and just take off, you won't be positioned or prepared as well as the others in the race who properly used their prep steps. You might just give them an upper hand. Properly following the steps, you'll be well prepared by the time the horn sounds.

Once you hear the command, "Go!" you take off, and the race has begun. The principles in this book will demonstrate that failure isn't the end of the race for you. It really might just signal the beginning . . . or at least a new beginning. It's time to get off the ground, to shake yourself, to renew your thinking, and to get back in the race again!

2

Don't Blame Delilah

Sometimes, in the most uncomfortable situations where we find ourselves, one of the easiest things to do is to begin to play the blame game. This is natural and usually understandable. It brings some kind of misunderstood, false peace to be able to believe that "it's your fault I am where I am." I think there are places and times in life we all do it. Fatherless sons blame absentee fathers, divorcees blame ex-spouses, blacks blame whites, women blame men, unattractive folks blame attractive folks, obese folks blame skinny folks, and so on. It somehow comforts us emotionally to believe that if it weren't for a particular person, place, or thing, we wouldn't be in this predicament. To be totally fair, there is no denying the influencers that help or encourage us to make the decisions we sometimes make. Yet, in reality, each decision we make in life is just that—a decision we made!

The opposite of the blame game is personal responsibility. Chuck Gallozzi said, "When we take responsibility, we admit we are the ones responsible for the choices we make. We, not other people or events, are responsible for the way we think and feel. It is our life, and we are in charge of it. We are free to enjoy or disdain it. No, we are not responsible for all that happens to us, but we are responsible for how we think, feel, and act when they happen."

I realize that's a heavy statement, but it carries a heavy truth as well. I think it's a necessary step in removing yourself from what I call the victim mentality. That mentality says, "Outside of my control, something was done to me." It's quite easy to view life through that lens. Doing so doesn't require taking a personal look at self. Please understand that I am in no way denying the reality of circumstances and situations we experience that are totally beyond our control. For instance, a molested child clearly did nothing to bring that experience on herself. Someone who walks into a bank and finds himself involved in a bank robbery didn't plan that event for the day. So, in that type of situation, immediately after the initial experience, it might be too early to attempt to combat the victim mentality. The one who experiences such is obviously a victim.

However, in the events or times that follow the initial experience, we have to address the victim mentality. For instance, in the above quote, Chuck says, "We are not responsible for all that happens to us, but we are responsible for how we think, feel, and act when they happen." No one would deny that African-Americans experienced roughly one hundred years of slavery. You would imagine, in a century, that one acquires certain attitudes, thought processes, and ways of life. If you live in a certain environment for an extended period, you will begin to pick up habits and proclivities of those whom you live around. Yet, at some point after your release, you have to go back to question if your thought pattern is sincerely your thought pattern or a result of the environment where you spent so much time. Today, African-Americans are forced to decide if we want to acknowledge every hurdle in life as "the man just trying to keep us down" or to see if we have done all we can to break the glass ceiling.

I often hear confessions made that a childhood molestation caused one to go down the path of homosexuality. Actually, I've made the claim that childhood molestation was the cause of my heterosexual promiscuity. Because I was molested as a child, I grew up with a fear of being gay. Therefore, I had an unquenchable desire to chase (or be caught) by every woman I came across. Did the molestation happen? Yes. Was it a motivator for why I had so many sexual experiences with women whom I sometimes had very little relationship with? Yes. But could it be the sole source for having an illegal sexual relationship with a woman today? No. Here is where I begin to deal with the victim mentality within myself. I've stopped saying, "I am the way I am because of what happened to me then." The reality of the past is real. The knowledge or understanding of its bondage is real. Yet the opportunity for help to overcome is equally real. Today's doors and choices are before you. It is now your difficult decision to choose which door you want to enter. Don't continue to be a victim; instead, be the victor.

Remember, the victim mentality says because you were a victim, your attitude or thought process was bequeathed to you by another. It says, "I can't help the way I feel because of what was done to me." Personal responsibility says you have to tilt your head and view the situation differently. It sounds like this: "Yes, you did what you did to me, but I choose to search for the area under my control that allowed this to be. I choose to stop giving you an opportunity to continue misleading me. Yes, you divorcing me hurt, but I initially chose to marry you. Yes, your betrayal hurt me, but I chose to allow you into my life. Yes, you did expose my secrets, but I chose to share them with you."

It doesn't say things are my fault, but I won't deny my responsibility in the situation.

Denying my part in the picture continually robs me of authority and power that I have. I will not continue to leave the power of my freedom and my progress in the hands of another. If everything is always someone else's fault, they control where I stand now. Today, that ends. I choose to be the master of my destiny.

God's View of the Blame Game

Let's take a look at the first earthly failure to see how God views the blame game. The first recorded failure of man is in Genesis 3. Adam received specific instructions from God not to eat of the tree of the knowledge of good and evil. He told Adam that in the day he ate of the tree, he would surely die. As the account goes, Eve was deceived by the serpent and ate. After she ate, she gave to her husband, Adam and he ate. After the crime had been committed, God entered the story and questioned Adam.

> When the woman saw that the fruit of the tree was good for food and pleasing to the eye, and also desirable for gaining wisdom, she took some and ate it. She also gave some to her husband, who was with her, and he ate it. Then the eyes of both of them were opened, and they realized they were naked; so they sewed fig leaves together and made coverings for themselves. Then the man and

*his wife heard the sound of the LORD God as he was walking in the garden in the cool of the day, and they hid from the LORD God among the trees of the garden. But the LORD God called to the man, "Where are you?" He answered, "I heard you in the garden, and I was afraid because I was naked; so I hid." And he said, "Who told you that you were naked? Have you eaten from the tree that I commanded you not to eat from?" The man said, "**The woman you put here with me—she gave me some fruit from the tree, and I ate it.**" Then the LORD God said to the woman, "What is this you have done?" The woman said, "**The serpent deceived me**, and I ate."*

– Genesis 3:6-14 (Emphasis mine)

So the LORD God said to the serpent, "Because you have done this, cursed are you above all the livestock and all the wild animals! You will crawl on your belly and you will eat dust all the days of your life. And I will put enmity between you and the woman, and between your offspring and hers; he will crush your head, and you will strike his heel." To the woman he said, "I will greatly increase your pains in childbearing; with pain you will give birth to children. Your desire will be for your husband, and he will rule over you." To Adam he said, "Because you listened to your wife and ate from the tree about which I commanded you, 'You must not eat of it,' cursed is the ground because of you; through painful toil you will eat of it all the days of your life. It will produce thorns and thistles for you, and you will eat the plants of the

field. By the sweat of your brow you will eat your food until you return to the ground, since from it you were taken; for dust you are and to dust you will return."
— Genesis 3:14-19

There are very interesting results in this story. When God showed up to meet Adam, where they normally met, Adam wasn't there. Something was different. Adam's pattern had changed. God asked, "What's the problem?" and Adam basically said, "I'm ashamed to be with You right now because I see myself differently." God's reply is quite interesting. He said, "Nothing is different. You have been naked since your creation, but you weren't aware of it. Because you saw yourself through My eyes, your state never bothered you. It was not until you got a glimpse of yourself through eyes other than Mine that you found a reason to be ashamed. Who is describing what you look like?" Wow! That's a powerful concept!

Notice the sequence of events. The woman said it was the serpent's fault, so God punished the serpent. Adam said it was the woman's fault, so God punished the woman. Yet it all began with Adam, so Adam also had a price to pay. God's view of the blame game goes like this: Outside forces can influence us to make wrong decisions. When they do, influencers also have to pay consequences. Nevertheless, the ultimate decision still lies in the hands of the one given the main responsibility. In this case, that person was Adam.

There will always be influencers for right and wrong decisions. Be careful who you allow to be in your ear.

What About the Enemy?

It probably causes great problems for people to hear someone talk so much about personal responsibility in a world where people are so apt to blame the devil for everything. Am I denying the existence or influence of a real, live devil? Am I suggesting that he doesn't have a part to play in this? Certainly not. However, I don't have to go very far from our Genesis passage to see just how significant he is . . . or isn't.

We would not dare deny the presence of the enemy in the Genesis account, would we? After all, he's embodied in that crafty serpent, right? Many scholars contend that old serpent literally seduced Eve into taking a bite of that fruit. I will fight the temptation of many scholars to get into the debate of why Adam left his wife alone in the first place, mainly because I think the married readers probably already know. I don't think it is possible for anyone to love his wife more than I love mine. But just imagine having the entire world practically to yourselves all day, every day. I can hear the world's first husband saying one day, "Sweetheart, it's been great talking to you and only you every single day. But today, I think I'll go hang out with the elephants and flies for a little bit. I will be back by dinner time." Call it what you will, but let's be real!

Here's what I want you to notice. The Bible says that the serpent was crafty. It doesn't speak of any physical strength. That word, "crafty," speaks of a devious ability to deceive a person. That means his power isn't physical; it's mental. He simply engaged her mind. He got into her head. In turn, the same is basically true concerning what Eve did to Adam. She didn't tie him down and force him to eat. It was a war of the mind, and the first parents lost them both. This brings me to an uncomfortable point. The power of the enemy is often internal or within me.

The Enemy "In-a-Me"!

The more contemporary way of saying it is, "The enemy is in-a-me!" While millions spend time running around claiming, "The devil made me do it!" I don't always think so. I'll pause here to tell a joke I heard concerning this. To the really spiritual folks, please don't be offended by a parenthetical break. One day satan was sitting outside God's office, crying hysterically. As the angels passed him on their way to see and to report to God, one of them asked him, "Why are you crying so?" satan responded, "I'm really going to get in trouble when I go in there." "Why?" the angel asked. satan replied, "Because those people are in there, and they're blaming me for everything!" I have a feeling that truth won't be very far from this joke!

While it can't be denied that satan is an enemy of mankind, I don't see where he's been given power to force us to do anything. Come on, be honest. Just think of any sin you have committed. Did the devil *make* you say it? Did the devil *make* you touch it? Did the devil *make* you feel it, or did he encourage you to do so? Were you uncontrollably forced to touch the untouchable? I can't think of one sin I've ever committed that didn't have my own decision attached to it. Sometimes I felt justified in my actions. Sometimes I felt that people had pushed certain buttons and forced me to release my anger in words. However, it was never really anyone else's fault. It was always a choice.

Here's a little exercise I use to illustrate my point. This works really well with the people who battle with temper issues, people who feel they simply can't always control their tongues and what comes up comes out. I always say, "If you can't control your tongue when people hit certain buttons and you have to respond, would you have to give a response if it were to a gang member who was pointing a gun in your face?" If you would have the ability to hold your peace then, you have the ability to hold it anytime. It's just a matter of making a choice to do so. I'm not saying that it's easy. I'm just saying that, ultimately, it's always a choice.

Because of certain experiences in college, I remember thinking I had no control over sexual appetites. Because of a great depression I experienced from losing my brother, I felt that any woman who reached for me had a right to have me, over any decision of my own. I felt I had no power to say, "No." It really got bad at one point. I recall my breaking point. It was at the close of one illegal experience. My roommate, Lamont (who preaches the gospel also now), came in the room and found me on the floor, pretending to be sick. He jokingly yelled at me, "Get yo' butt up off the floor. You know nothing's wrong with you! She's already left anyway!" That was the point when I knew things were way out of control. I couldn't seem to stop myself from having sex with people, but I would feel so awful afterward that I just wanted to be alone and bathe in depression.

Could I have said "no"? Absolutely. I just couldn't seem to find the strength or will to do so. I realize there are others who feel that same way now. Here's a thought. If you thought that having an encounter would cost you your very life in that instant, would you be able to resist? If so, you can resist anytime. Once again, it's a matter of choice. I'm not saying it's easy but that it's possible.

> But each one is tempted when, by his own evil desire, he is dragged away and enticed. Then, after desire has been conceived, it gives birth to sin; and sin, when it is fullgrown, gives birth to death.
> —James 1:14-15

James recorded a process of how things happen concerning temptation. What's interesting is he never even mentioned the devil, but he did mention the "enemy." I stress that because I believe the "enemy" is "in-a-me"! James said that when the evil desire that already exists in you is enticed, you're pulled away from the right thing. See, there's something already within me that looks for an opportunity to do wrong. You may not always notice it because it's not always stirred. Remember the Adam and Eve story? How could Eve disobey God when sin hadn't even come into the world? At least we have the benefit of being able to blame things on the sin nature we inherit from Adam and Eve's fall. We often hear that they were perfect or without sin. In actuality, I believe they were mature without *realized* or *manifested* sin. It hadn't been stirred or released yet. Even Paul concluded, "There is no good thing within me." (See Romans 7:18.) Most contend that the reason that nothing good is in the flesh is because Adam placed or brought bad things into the flesh. The problem with that is we see a bad desire coming from his flesh before sin was even realized.

> *The weapons we fight with are not the weapons of the world. On the contrary, they have divine power to demolish strongholds. We demolish arguments and every pretension that sets itself up against the knowledge of God, and we take captive every thought to make it obedient to Christ. And we will be ready to punish every act of*

disobedience, once your obedience is complete.
—*II Corinthians 10:46*

James said after the desire has conceived, it births sin. Following that, sin births death of some sort. Not limited to physical death, it could be spiritual, emotional, financial, or other types.

Do you see the process here? Just imagine a pregnant mother who gives birth to a child. We all know that if a mother gave birth this morning, she didn't conceive last night. That's not possible. The process takes time, as does the death or sin process. It all begins with an evil desire that is within self. When that desire gets to jump around and play in our minds, sin soon after follows. If there is any power to be given to the enemy (in-a-me), it's that of being allowed to linger in our minds. Permitting things to fester in our minds gives room for strongholds to develop. Once a stronghold develops, we often feel that we have no choice but to carry out the act.

You Are Not the First!

The problematic person inside wasn't just a problem for Adam. It was a problem for Samson also. Notice:

The woman gave birth to a boy and named him Samson. He grew and the LORD blessed him, and the Spirit of the LORD began to stir him while he was in Mahaneh Dan, between

> *Zorah and Eshtaol. Samson went down to Timnah and saw there a young Philistine woman. When he returned, he said to his father and mother, "I have seen a Philistine woman in Timnah; now get her for me as my wife."*
>
> *—Judges 13:23-14:2*

This will be somewhat intriguing to those who have heard the often-told tale of Samson and Delilah. Many probably know how the story ends. It's an embarrassing end with Samson being laughed at by his enemies and having his power stripped by the ever-so-persistent Delilah. I want you to realize that Delilah wasn't Samson's problem, ever. Samson's problem was always Samson!

> *His father and mother replied, "Isn't there an acceptable woman among your relatives or among all our people? Must you go to the uncircumcised Philistines to get a wife?" But Samson said to his father, "Get her for me. She's the right one for me." (His parents did not know that this was from the LORD, who was seeking an occasion to confront the Philistines; for at that time they were ruling over Israel.)*
>
> *—Judges 14:3-4*

In verse 24 of chapter 13, Samson was born. Three verses later, when we hear him speak for the first time, his words aren't about how powerful God is. His words aren't about finding and fulfilling destiny. His words are not even about the deliverance of his people. The initial words we hear from his mouth are: "I want a woman, and you need to get her for me!" The priority of Samson that the Bible chooses to reveal to us is Samson's proclivity to women. We are not discussing the right or the wrong of his actions, just the blatant truth of them.

In spite of all the prophetic words spoken over his life, in spite of the divine intervention concerning his birth, once born, Samson had a strong desire for something that seemed to have nothing to do with his God given purpose here on earth – women. Unfortunately, I fear that many men understand his problem. This in no way suggests that all men walk out these actions as Samson did or even feel them to the degree that Samson felt them. Yet I would contend that most men understand to some degree. After all, some men have no attraction toward women at all. Some men discover their attractions are turned inward toward other men, power, success, or other things altogether. While the object of their affection may be different, something often gains the attention (if only mentally) of men.

> On the fourth day, they said to Samson's wife, "Coax your husband into explaining the riddle for us, or we will burn you and your father's household to death. Did you invite us here to rob us?" Then Samson's wife threw herself on him, sobbing, "You hate me! You don't really love me. You've given my people a riddle, but you haven't told me the answer."
> —Judges 14:15-16

While Samson was arguably the strongest man physically on the planet, he was certainly Clark Kent in the emotional department. Just a few tears and several complaints from the object of his affection, and this picture of strength suddenly became putty.

> *"I haven't even explained it to my father or mother," he replied, "so why should I explain it to you?" She cried the whole seven days of the feast. So on the seventh day he finally told her, because she continued to press him. She in turn explained the riddle to her people.*
> *—Judges 14:16-17*

While most know of Samson's fate at the hands of Delilah, we can see his weakness with his first wife, who is given no name. After Samson killed a lion with his bare hands, he left a riddle for the townspeople to solve. When they realized they were unable to do so, they approached Samson's wife, who was obviously more loyal to her people than to her husband. After she pressured Samson, he gave in. He was so angry with her that he sent her back to her father after the ordeal. However, by then the damage was done and his weakness revealed. Samson fell hard, fell fast and generally fell wrong!

By the time Delilah came along in chapter 16, the door of Samson's vulnerability was already obvious.

My point is simply this. It isn't fair to blame Delilah and her cunningness for Samson's downfall. Delilah did not discover Samson's weakness by magic. She didn't physically torture Samson into telling her where the secret of his strength lay. She simply walked through the door of his heart. Now, many could look at this in a multiplicity of ways, but the cold truth is that Delilah simply used the information she received from Samson against him. It would be futile for Samson to spend his years thinking, *"If it weren't for that darn Delilah, I would never have been in this predicament!"* A better statement would be: *"If I hadn't given in to Delilah, I would never have been in this predicament!"* There will always be adversaries and opponents clawing and fighting to discover our weaknesses and vulnerabilities. The good news is that they can't have what we don't give them.

> *Some time later, he fell in love with a woman in the Valley of Sorek whose name was Delilah. The rulers of the Philistines went to her and said, "See if you can lure him into showing you the secret of his great strength and how we can overpower him so we may tie him up and subdue him. Each one of us will give you eleven hundred shekels of silver."*
>
> *–Judges 16:4-5 (NIV)*

I titled this chapter, "Don't Blame Delilah," for more than one reason. I hope those reasons have been clearly outlined for you. Just in case they haven't, allow me to provide one more reason. It's difficult to place blame of your mishaps on something you sought out! That's right! Delilah did not approach Samson; Samson approached Delilah. The Bible says he fell in love with her. Isn't that always the problem? We have to watch what we love. Some people say you can't help what you love. I say, "You had better!" It's quite easy to attach yourself to things that will destroy you or rob you of your purpose.

> *Above all else, guard your heart, for it is the wellspring of life.*
> — *Proverbs* 4:23

Many times in life, it's not the adversarial opponents that come into our lives that strip us of our destiny. God wouldn't allow that to be. The trouble is how we end up feeling about it after the war is over. Certainly, God's plan for your life is bigger than any giant, devil, Delilah, or any Samsonite issue you could ever face. The problem is we often leave the battle so scarred and robbed of self-confidence that we fail to want to go on. That was Samson's real problem, not the weakness of his heart. I say that because God is such a merciful, forgiving God that He provides multiple opportunities for us to please Him. I've never believed in a one-shot type of God. He is too wise and understands the frailty of men too well to be like that. He will always allow the hair of the repentant sinner to grow again. However, while God forgives the failure of a repentant heart, the question is, is that heart able to forgive itself? You and I have seasons, struggles, and problems that we sometimes trip over. I want to encourage you to keep getting back up. When you can't get up, you start sounding like Samson in his final prayer, which asked, "Let me die here." But just like He did for Samson, God can do even more in your life after a failure. But you don't have to let that be your final act. Allow God to keep using you to get glory for His name.

> But the hair on his head began to grow again after it had been shaved. . . . Then Samson prayed to the LORD, "O Sovereign LORD, remember me. O God, please strengthen me just once more, and let me with one blow get revenge on the Philistines for my two eyes." Then Samson reached toward the two central pillars on which the temple stood. Bracing himself against them, his right hand on one and his left hand on the other, Samson said, "Let me die with the Philistines!" Then he pushed with all his might, and down came the temple on the rulers and all the people in it. Thus he killed many more when he died than while he lived.
>
> *—Judges 16:2, 28-30*

I took the long way around the barnyard to say, "The devil didn't make you do it!" As he did with Adam and Eve, he may have made it look appealing, irresistible, and necessary, but he didn't *make* you do it. He couldn't! He doesn't have that kind of power.

Now, once you can admit that he didn't make us do it, you can agree that he can't make us keep doing it. Therefore, if it's not him, it must be us! So I don't have to spend my time trying to figure out how to defeat him, because Christ already did that. He's already defeated. I need to spend time figuring out how to defeat or conquer myself! I have to discover how to get back to seeing myself as God sees me. I may be naked, but I don't have to be ashamed. Why not? Because I've always been naked. God knew my nakedness. Once I can get back to viewing myself through God's eyes, the opinions of others will lose strength.

3

Give No More Power!

I have a slight infatuation with the show *MTV Cribs*. It excites me to see the amazing homes where people live (or sometimes pretend to live). Generally, each episode will include a segment with the celebrity also showing his or her cars. They virtually take us through the garage and flash a Rolls Royce, a Lamborghini, a high-end Mercedes, or some other beautiful, exotic, and *expensive* car. This morning, I woke with a very strange image in mind.

No More Fuel

As fabulous as those cars are, with all they accurately (or sometimes inaccurately) represent, this morning I awoke with the image of a Rolls Royce Phantom on the side of the road simply because it ran out of gas. I know that's a stretch, but it serves well for this illustration. Other cars were zooming by. Some were extravagant, and some were just hoopties. Never-the-less, they were all passing the celebrated car that sat on the side of the road because it had no gas.

Now, I must admit that was a strange image to have, but I got the point. No matter how fabulous, exotic, or expensive a car is, it still needs fuel to be considered transportation. No matter how wonderful it may look on the inside, it can't get you where you want to go unless you continue to feed it fuel. In the same breath, what you don't feed can't get you there!

No More Fire

I remember the last house I lived in before I left Indiana to move here to Georgia. The house was right behind Ben Davis High School (of which I am a proud '91 graduate). I loved that house. It was the first house I had with a fireplace. Sometimes, I would light the fireplace just to stare at the fire. Call it strange, but it's what I did sometimes. I remember days watching the raging blaze begin to calm to a mild simmer, at which point I would simply add a log or two, give a little poke, and within minutes the fire was raging again. Without more wood, the fire would soon die, but as long as I continued to feed it, it would burn and burn. Fire is one of the necessary elements of life, yet it must have something to consume or it cannot survive. When it has enough materials to consume, a small fire can become a citywide, raging inferno. However, if it lacks consumable substance, a flame can be stomped out by a child! What determines the difference is if it is fed or not.

At the time I write this section, I'm nearing the end of one year and standing at the door of the next. At this time of year, people generally spend time giving reflective thoughts to the year that has passed. As you probably know from reading this book, my life two years ago was next to overwhelming! I moved to a new city, where I hardly knew anyone. My wife and I spent several months apart. Then we spent the time together like two strangers meeting for the first time. Other family members didn't quite know what to think of my actions, so not a whole lot was said. Former church members found themselves trying to decide whether to judge my actions harshly and condemn me or to stand patiently in agreement for my total restoration. To put it plainly, it has been a rough two years, the roughest years I have ever seen!

However, what I found most interesting is why it was so difficult. It wasn't just because of the mistakes I made. After all, that was quite some time ago. The years were so difficult because of the continual rehearsal of mistakes in my own mind. The residue of my mistakes continued to make the time difficult for me.

Oftentimes we hear a lot of information about house fires and the people who die in them or are rescued from them. But here's something you may not have known. It is estimated that 50 to 80 percent of fire deaths are the result of smoke inhalation rather than burns. In other words, it's not always the fire that kills but the smoke. So you could be rescued from a burning building yet have the residue of the experience rob you of life.

More often than not, I think that's the common experience of the day. I believe many times people survive difficult situations and circumstances. Yet the rehearsing of the circumstances in their mind keeps them from being able to move forward. There are women who have survived being in abusive relationships. However, it is possible to be rescued from the abuser yet carry the victim mentality within oneself. In cases like those, victims treat every new acquaintance as a potential abuser. So they end up chasing away people who have the ability and desire to help and to heal them. They are no longer in the fire, but the smoke is killing them.

For each of us who have experienced traumatic situations in the last year, there is a very challenging task ahead for us. The task is to avoid carrying our yesterday into our tomorrow, even if our "yesterday" experience just ended this morning.

Honestly, that won't be the easiest of things to do. Sometimes it's very difficult to let go of the past. At times it's difficult to desire to let things go, even painful things. You would think we would have a speedy desire to release things that hurt, but even that can be difficult.

In spite of the difficulty, this is the decision you and I must make if we plan to move forward in the coming days. To refuse to make a conscious decision to do so is to decide to stay stuck in the muck and mire of yesterday.

If you think like I often do, you're probably saying something like, "Okay, it sounds good to hear someone say to stop fueling the fire, but how am I supposed to do that? How am I supposed to stop thinking about something so attached to me?" That's an excellent question. In all honesty, I had to launch a major search for the answer. It wasn't something just ringing as a reality for me. I began searching the Internet for help.

I wasn't researching information for this book, either. I was searching for help for myself. See, this book wasn't just written to be a help to you. It was written to express my personal journey. I empathize with you on a far deeper level than most, for I know the pain of trying to release the mistakes of my past as they desperately hold on to me. In this particular case, I'm touched with the feeling of your infirmity.

Based on that reality, I began a desperate search for information by other writers on the subject of moving beyond a failure. A lot of writers spoke of distractions. They listed things like: go to a movie, listen to music, or read a book.

Really? I free myself of repetitive negative thoughts by reading a book? Dude, I *wrote* a book and was not completely distracted from the uncomfortable thoughts! Sometimes listening to music created a relaxing ambience for my nagging thoughts. Television seemed a wonderful distraction until the programs ended. Then my thoughts, like a schoolyard bully, seemed to smile at me just to remind me, "We're still here!" One day I sat in front of the television for countless hours. Yes, I was distracted, but by the end of the day, my brain felt like absolute mush. In that case, I think the cure was worse than the problem.

All jesting aside, follow the step that works best for you. Different things will empower you to move forward. I will discuss what works for me and will allow you to be your own judge. In order to do that, I have to use a verse of Scripture you'll see often throughout this book. Let's turn to the text in Philippians.

> *Brethren, I count not myself to have apprehended: but this one thing I do, forgetting those things which are behind, and reaching forth unto those things which are before, I press toward the mark for the prize of the high calling of God in Christ Jesus.*
> — *Philippians 3:13-14 (KJV)*

While I am using this passage of Scripture outside the context in which it was written, I will maintain the integrity of the text.

In the verses referenced above, the writer said that while he had not arrived at his main goal yet, there was one thing he did. Although he spoke of "one thing," he mentioned three: forgetting, reaching, and pressing. At times one goal may require several steps.

Step one focuses on forgetting. My feeling is that most people arrive at the entirely wrong conclusion when it comes to the idea of forgetting in this verse. When asking others of their opinions of what forgetting means, the answers often sound like the idea is for a person to be no longer aware of the thing to be forgotten. While it makes total sense as to why one would think that way, I'm not really sure that's a human possibility. See, the human brain is more amazing than any computer ever created. It has the ability to store incredible amounts of information. You do not go back to the manufacturer every six months for an upgrade, either! The mind typically remembers everything. Even things you are not consciously aware of are often accessed with little effort. Have you smelled an aroma that recalled something from years earlier? Many of us have heard songs that took us back decades and unlocked memories we had well tucked away. That's because the mind doesn't forget in that sense. It just stores.

So what did Paul mean by "forgetting what is behind?" I believe what Paul was encouraging us to do was not to become unaware of certain events but rather not to be paralyzed by them. It's not that you can remove hurtful events you have experienced, but you can stop them from hindering your forward progress.

If you have experienced a painful divorce, which has caused you to lose your trust in the words of people, you may not be able to undo the divorce, but you can work at containing that lack of trust to the specific individual and not spreading it to everyone you come across. Sometimes our experiences affect us in such a way that we are not able to get beyond them easily. Something that happened five, ten, or twenty years ago should not have the authority to continue controlling your life today! Getting the ability to move forward is a type of forgetting. It's not that you're no longer aware of what happened to you; it's just that you won't be held captive by it!

Okay, so your next question is, "How am I supposed to do that?" I believe the answer lies in the next step of

Paul's statement. Linking it to forgetting, he mentioned reaching. This suggests it may be difficult to walk out of one thing when you're not consciously walking toward something else. While forgetting may be the initial step, it's not the entire focus. It is just one piece in the puzzle of reaching the goal! Don't get the priorities out of place.

Rearview Mirrors

Any of us who have ever sat behind the wheel of a car knows the importance of a rearview mirror. It would be quite difficult to reach any destination without glancing into it at least once. It makes you aware of the traffic or objects that are behind you. Sometimes things are coming at you from behind, and your rearview mirror makes you aware of the approach and enables you to protect yourself accordingly. As significant as rearview mirrors are, they can't be your primary driving tools. They are just one of the pieces. Your main attention is on what is ahead, not what's behind. We often take a quick glance into the things behind to check for trouble and then keep looking ahead. Anyone who places too much time and attention on his rearview mirror is one who is sure to have an accident! In other words, your yesterday is just that—yesterday. Be mindful of it; be aware of it. But don't be led by it. Being led today by your yesterday is like someone in a car using only rearview mirrors.

The Goal Is Ahead!

Here is a question you need to answer. What are you reaching for? What are you chasing after? Even after a major failure, downfall, mistake, or disappointment, you need to have something you are reaching after. I'll suggest that the "goal" shouldn't even be just surviving the failure, because that still has the most attention on yesterday. If you've experienced a divorce, your primary goal should not be just surviving. Perhaps you see beyond just surviving to reaching a place where you're happy again. If you've experienced a bankruptcy, the goal shouldn't be just being able to hold up your head without shame. Perhaps it should be buying a home or paying off a car loan. The focus needs to be on what's up the road and not just what's behind you. This is the thing we should be reaching after.

Without something to reach after, we find it more difficult to forget what's behind. Remember those high-school-days heartbreaks? Some of mine are pretty funny now. However, they were absolutely devastating then! What's funny is how heartbroken I would be from being dumped by someone. However, that devastation somehow didn't seem so crushing once I learned that someone else found me interesting! The pain of yesterday seemed to dim in the light and possibility of tomorrow. Now, I'm not suggesting that you run out to look for a new relationship. Nonetheless, I am suggesting that you begin to place the attention on what you're moving toward rather than on what you've come through!

Get Ready to Press

I hope I haven't given you the impression that leaving yesterday behind will be a simple task. If I have, then maybe you should revisit the Philippians text with me. Notice the third step in Paul's "one thing" was to press. First, forget; second, reach; then, press! I believe it's no coincidence that he wrote these words.

Even though you've made a decision to move beyond the pains of yesterday, even though you've decided to reach for the promise of tomorrow, you'll still have to determine to be relentless. Success has its price. I doubt that many would say it comes easy. So after you've determined to go after it, you'll have to develop a relentless stick-to-itiveness to reach your goals. Some days of moving forward will seem easier than others. Other days will be quite challenging. That's where the press needs to come in. You have to make a decision to continue moving forward even when it feels like success is eluding you. That will be the determining factor or the answer to the question, "How bad do you want it?"

How can you protect yourself from things that will make you want to give up the press? Whom must you avoid to stay focused? What things must you feast on to keep up the motivation to press ahead? The answers

71 | P a g e

are different for each of us but still need to be figured out. Only you know the sins and the weights that so easily beset you!

I recall old segments of weight-training shows on television. Two or three guys would be involved. One man would lift the weights, and another would be spotting and encouraging. Somewhere around the last repetition, the lifter would begin to lose strength. As he'd slowly lift the weights the last time, the spotter would be yelling, "C'mon! You can do it! Give me all ya got! Give me all ya got!" Sometimes, the only way you can get that last lift out is to give it all you have. You have to put everything on the line to complete the goal. Stop giving fuel to the things that keep you from your goal, and give your all to completing the goal. You've had the right stuff all the time. Now, it's time to put the right stuff in the right place! Let's get it done!

4 Choices, Challenges and Changes

I'm amazed that God provided me the strength to write this book at the time I did so. I was completely overwhelmed with enormous depression, swimming in a sea of doubts and fears, and totally questioning my ability or desire to continue moving forward in ministry. I'm not at all ashamed to express that, because I sense that many of you reading now have often felt that way. I wondered if God was still with me. In spite of all the Scripture we read, confess, and believe about His constant presence, I questioned if that applied in my situation.

What would possibly be able to make a person

with a ministry history like mine ask such questions? Surely, this couldn't have been the first time in my life I committed a sin, could it? After all, I was operating in ministry before I was ten years old. Didn't I have shortcomings, missteps, or mistakes before reaching my thirties? Absolutely! But something was different this time. It wasn't just the sin of adultery, though that's big enough to make your average sincere Christian step back and take a second look at the calling. It wasn't the greater number of people discussing my moral failure, although the number was much greater this time than times before. In reality, it wasn't the external parts at all that caused such ruckus inside. It was the internal pieces that created such turmoil. See, this time, there was something different about me! I wasn't the same kid I was when I made a similar mistake some ten years earlier. This time, I had come to such a greater place in my relationship and awareness of God that disappointing Him wasn't as trivial a matter as it had seemed in the past.

What I had come to realize was that because my relationship with Him had become stronger and more solid, it wasn't as easy to stand on disobedient ground and feel justified about it.

You would think that a greater relationship with God would cause you to feel even more forgiven than you did in the past when you had less knowledge. It does, should, and did. But we haven't gotten to that part yet. At the time of writing, I was operating on a misunderstood interpretation of "everyone to whom much is given, from him much will be required" (Luke 12:48, NKJV).

It was not a comfortable place to be. I should have known better. Truthfully, I *did* know better. It was more painful to me to display such an error because my love for God was much stronger than before. I'll try to paint a better picture through an example I frequently use with Bible study students.

Remember being a child and hearing your mother say, "All right, it will be dinnertime soon, so don't eat any of the cookies in the cookie jar. You'll ruin your dinner." As a disobedient child, the fear was always getting caught and having to deal with the consequences of disobedience. The whole time I was sneaking a cookie out, I thought of the painful repercussions I'd encounter if I got caught. Fear was the motivator, not enough to steer me in the right direction but just enough to cause me to be as secretive as I possibly could be. I was always aware that getting caught would not bring joyful consequences.

Fast-forward several years to adult life. I still occasionally get instructions from my mother that are against my personal desires, but the act of obedience comes from a different emotion now. I'm not afraid of getting caught and reaping physical consequences. After all, my mother has passed the age of being able to catch me physically now. Sorry, Mom, but I'm finally faster and stronger than you☺. I'm not motivated to obey her out of fear. I'm now motivated out of love. I simply don't want to disappoint her. Knowing that I've let her down creates a disappointment in me that is almost unbearable. In other words, I didn't always used to obey; I was just sneaky. Today, I have a desire to please her. I want to make her smile, and when I don't, I'm devastated.

That is what makes committing gross sin so difficult for me today. It's not that I don't know I'm forgiven even before I fail. It's that I have a heart desire to make God smile. Feeling as if I've made Him frown is distressing.

If pleasing God is so important to those of us who often fail to do so, the question has to be: Why don't we? You could take the popular route and just say, "The devil made me do it," but I'm sure you've read enough by now to know that excuse won't get very far with me. No, it literally comes down to the choices we make. Heaven knows there could be a plethora of reasons or motivators for those choices. Nevertheless, it all begins there.

I have to admit, I've often wondered why God didn't intervene in certain situations and just prevent me from doing something stupid. Honestly, sometimes He did. But I wanted Him to be the kind of guardian that would physically block me every time I seemed to veer off the proper path. I would be on my way somewhere I had no business being, anticipating a flat tire before reaching my destination. Or I would expect an unexpected phone call to come through to change my plans completely. I literally waited on God to appear like a watchful big brother and utter the words, "Uh, uh, uh," or "No, no, no you don't!" I literally spent years with that kind of expectation of God. Okay, who am I kidding? I still do that!

Now I understand that's not how God wants to operate. That would remove part of the glory He gave to us as His prized creation. Look at the creation of man to see God's plan.

> *Then God said, "Let us make man in our image, in our likeness, and let them rule over the fish of the sea and the birds of the air, over the livestock, over all the earth, and over all the creatures that move along the ground." So God created man in his own image, in the image of God he created him; male and female he created them.*
> *–Genesis 1:26-27*

God's desire was to make man in His own image and likeness. While there are those people who believe that image and likeness speaks of physical characteristics, I'll present a different argument. I don't think we resemble God in a physical way at all. Just viewing other portions of Scripture prove that.

> *God is spirit, and His worshipers must worship in spirit and in truth.*
> *–John 4:24*

No one has ever seen God, but God the One and Only, who is at the Father's side, has made him known.
–John 1:18

He is the image of the invisible God, the firstborn over all creation.
–Colossians 1:15

Who alone is immortal and who lives in unapproachable light, whom no one has seen or can see. To him be honor and might forever. Amen.
–I Timothy 6:16

Look at my hands and my feet. It is I myself! Touch me and see; a ghost does not have flesh and bones, as you see I have.
–Luke 24:39

Now to the King eternal, immortal, invisible, the only God, be honor and glory forever and ever. Amen.
–I Timothy 1:17

The Scriptures clearly outline the point that God is a spirit and that spirits don't have flesh and blood. God is the invisible God, which no man can see. So if the image and likeness that God bestowed on us were physical, He clearly missed the mark!

No, that likeness wasn't to be physical. It was something much deeper. Immediately following Adam's creation, God showed what that likeness was really designed to be.

> *God blessed them and said to them, "Be*
> *fruitful and increase in number; fill the earth*
> *and subdue it. Rule over the fish of the sea and*
> *the birds of the air and over every living*
> *creature that moves on the ground."*
>
> *—Genesis 1:28*

God created man to have authority over all natural things, including himself. He never intended for us to exist as little robots with no will, desire, or thought process of our own. That's probably a hard concept for most of us to comprehend because of how the human psyche works. Speaking personally, I'm not so sure if I want my children to have free will. I don't know if I'd have given my spouse free will. I definitely don't think I would have given my staff free will. If I were in charge of things, everything under my control would simply perform my will, exactly to my specifications. I wouldn't run the risk of being disappointed. I'm pretty confident that most of you will agree with me. If you knew your child was taking the car keys to go immediately to a dangerous place, would you hand him or her the keys this evening? Probably not. Yet the perfect love of God desires to be loved, honored, and respected by choice, not force or demand. That's one of the attributes of God that makes Him so difficult to understand with the human mind. So we have to approach God through faith and not senses.

With that in mind, we really can't blame God for the situations we find ourselves in. The argument of many atheists is, "If there is a God, why do children starve?" That's a good question, but I believe it's similar to the question that God asks us. "If you are such compassionate people, why are you so wasteful when there are so many starving children?" Is it God's fault, or is it ours? Is it God's fault that great numbers of people are murdered every year, or is it ours? Is it God's fault that the ozone layer of our planet is being destroyed, or is it ours? Is it God's fault that more than 50 percent of marriages end in divorce, or is it ours? I think you get the point.

Take a hard, serious look at your situation and answer honestly. Whatever mistake you made, didn't it begin with your own decision or choice to do so? I don't think this is the place where we build a fortress around ourselves, break out our dunce hats, and conclude that we're just a waste of air, but I do believe honesty is the first step to being healed, truly forgiven, and restored.

> *This day I call heaven and earth as witnesses against you that I have set before you life and death, blessings and curses. Now **choose** life, so that you and your children may live and that you may love the LORD your God, listen to his voice, and hold fast to him. For the LORD is your life, and he will give you many years in the land he swore to give to your fathers, Abraham, Isaac and Jacob.*
> *–Deuteronomy 30:19-20 (Emphasis mine)*

God provides each of us with an ability to choose what we want to do with the life that has been given to us. Unlike many, I don't believe that people are simply where they are with no personal input. On an ultimate level, a choice or decision has to be made. Even if you're born with money, you have to decide to keep it! The prodigal son of Luke 15 was certainly born into some level of wealth, but he chose to lose it. Again, I am in no way suggesting that life doesn't provide us with many motivators for the directions we take. However, we all must come to the firm conclusion that those directions are ultimately products of our own choices.

There's an amazing turn that becomes available once that stance is taken. It sounds a little bit like this: "If it was my decision to get to this place, now I can make the choice to leave this place. It might be more difficult leaving than it was coming, but that authority or choice belongs to me. I don't have to stay in this predicament against my will. My circumstances have lied to me. I'm not helpless. I still have choices. Today is the day I am coming to myself."

Challenges

In the last section, we dealt with our individual ability to make choices. While that's empowering, I must provide you the entire picture. In order to do that, I'll now place your attention on the challenges of those right or better choices. Countless times, I've felt a deluge of frustration after watching some economic empowerment seminar. Before the conclusion, I'd have the rushing feeling of shouting, "I can do that!" And generally, I could. Yet don't think for a second that any progressive decision is going to come without a challenge or two. It's great to make a wise decision to move forward. In actuality, it's necessary for most of us. Just prepare yourself that you will have a little bit of work to do. As the cliché says, "No pain, no gain." Many of us have already felt such pain from our negative decisions that we may not see the next few moves as pain but as necessary transformation.

I just want to prepare you mentally for the encounter up the road. This is a significant lesson. Many people get lost here because they believe that deciding to make a change is all that's necessary, but that's simply not always true. Just ask someone who has smoked cigarettes for years and discovers it's time to make a life-or-death decision to quit smoking. You would think that hearing the words, "stop smoking or die," would be all the rude awakening necessary to straighten up one's act, right?

So why is it that many continue to smoke after such a warning? Is it an astonishing amount of stubbornness? Is it pure defiance? Is it an absence of practicality? It could be all of the above. But it could be none of the above. That's right. The problem is sometimes none of those. At times the problem is in one not knowing how to follow through physically on a decision that has been made.

See, you can decide to do something that seems bodily impossible. Allow me to use an extreme physical example just to add color to my statement. Consider the physical condition of the man in John 5.

> Sometime later, Jesus went up to Jerusalem for a feast of the Jews. Now there is in Jerusalem near the Sheep Gate a pool, which in Aramaic is called Bethesda and which is surrounded by five covered colonnades. Here a great number of disabled people used to lie–the blind, the lame, the paralyzed. One who was there had been an invalid for thirty-eight years. When Jesus saw him lying there and learned that he had been in this condition for a long time, he asked him, "Do you want to get well?" "Sir," the invalid replied, "I have no one to help me into the pool when the water is stirred. While I am trying to get in, someone else goes down ahead of me." Then Jesus said to him, "Get up! Pick up your mat and walk." At once the man was cured; he picked up his mat and walked.
> –John 5:1-9

This man was a paralytic (suffered from paralysis, or the state of being paralyzed). Paralytic conditions are interesting in the sense that individuals have their limbs but they do not have the ability to use them. Wheelchair use of a person with no legs might not catch the curiosity of a child nearly as much as someone who has two legs that appear quite normal but simply are not functioning. Paralysis is the kind of problem that gives public results but has a hidden source.

I can imagine this man's frustration climbing to new

heights as Jesus absurdly asked him, "Do you want to be well?" He explained to Jesus, "It's not that I want to be here. I just can't get my body to obey my mind. I think, Get up, but my body doesn't cooperate. I need someone else to help me do what I'm thinking." That's what paralysis is. The mind works fine, but the body doesn't obey. The mind says, "One foot in front of the other," but the body just doesn't comply. There's a great frustration for the person who sends signals from the command center (the mind) but gets disobedience or no reply from the foot soldiers (the body). In a naval crew, this sort of rebellion is called mutiny. I believe we sometimes face mutinies within ourselves. We think, pray, or declare we are going to forgive those who have offended us. However, when we see them, we hold on to our grudge and simply ignore them. We decide to declare a fast, yet we find ourselves walking to the refrigerator. We set a certain time for prayer. Yet we end up falling asleep. We've made a decision that our flesh isn't cooperating with.

I believe that's what the apostle Paul spoke of:

> *So I find this law at work: When I want to do good, evil is right there with me. For in my inner being I delight in God's law; but I see another law at work in the members of my body, waging war against the law of my mind and making me a prisoner of the law of sin at work within my members. What a wretched man I am! Who will rescue me from this body of death?*
> *–Romans 7:21-24*

It's an absolute "mutiny" situation when you, as the authority figure, give commands that are not strictly adhered to. You do understand that you are the authority figure of your life, right? Good.

Dealing with Those Obstacles

So how do we deal with "war in my members"? How do I handle my flesh refusing to cooperate with my desire? Well, let's follow the example of the man in John 5. Jesus' question, "Do you want to be well?" seems a little strange, but it's effective. Jesus was really just checking his mental capacity. We can position ourselves in the place of healing but not really desire it. "Why would anyone do that?" you ask. That happens because some things appear socially correct to do. Millions of people position themselves in churches every week while they have no intention of doing anything the preacher talks about. They don't plan to forgive others, they don't plan to try to learn to love their enemies, and they don't plan to attempt to learn to prefer others above themselves. So why do they go? Because for some, church is the "right thing" to do. There are people who spend great amounts of money for counselors, therapists, and life coaches who give information that the clients never seem to implement. So why spend the money? Because it's the "right" or "good" thing to do. It's not always that the individual is trying to fool others, either. Sometimes, he can even fool himself. You can do something so long that you convince yourself it's what you want when you really may not want it at all.

Jesus' question to the man allowed him an opportunity to assess his true desire. It's possible to be sick so long that being well frightens you. Some people have been on welfare so long that getting a job and being totally independent and responsible seems terrifying. There are those who have been in jail so long that they've become what is called "institutionalized." They are more comfortable being ordered what to do, when to do it, and how long to do it than to have to navigate with the "burden" of freedom.

To Jesus' question, the man answered with the classic answer from the blame game. "It's everyone else's fault!" In classic fashion, Jesus didn't even address his excuse. He simply ordered him to get up, pick up his mat, and go home. Verse 9 tells us the man was cured immediately. That brings us to the primary step in handling our hurdles.

You Need a Word

This section speaks greatly to your faith. As a spiritual leader, I place a great deal of priority on faith. The first step forward is having a word from God. Romans 10:17 states, **Consequently, faith comes from hearing the message, and the message is heard through the word of Christ.** Therefore, it's most important that you position yourself in a place to hear the words of Christ. You are going to need to hear them over and over again. A lot of untruths have been placed in your head and, therefore, in your spirit. You can't undo those things with clichés and old wives' tales. You need God's Word! Just running to hear one sermon from your favorite gospel preacher may not be enough. You have to saturate yourself with what God says about your situation. He's never said you have to remain stuck in a bad condition. He's never said you have to be a victim. Before you can act, you need a word! You might need to safeguard yourself for a while from those who speak negative things into you. I'm not saying you have to become a recluse, but until you reach a safe place–spiritually, emotionally, and mentally–separation might not be a bad idea, depending on your environment. A word from God is enlightening and empowering. You don't have to take my word for it; just look at what happened to the man in John 5 who received one.

Move in the Power of That Word

Did you notice that in verse 9, this man, who was full of excuses two verses ago, just got up? What happened? I'll tell you. He got his word! Once God's Word hits you, it enables you to do what you couldn't do two seconds ago. The Scriptures are full of situations where people were empowered to do what they found themselves helpless to do earlier. Some people reading right now are testimonies of this. They thought they would never be able to live without certain people, places, or things, but today they stand delivered, free, and stronger than ever.

I don't know how long you've waited to receive

your word, but I want to speak strength to your desire. Don't give up. This man waited thirty-eight years. What if he had stopped positioning himself in year thirty-seven? He may have missed his moment! He didn't, and you can't, either! I speak to your spirit that you will continue to fight a good fight until you reach the finish. Your word is near. Just like this man, once you receive your word, forget about the past thirty-eight years, and focus on the present. Just get up! It doesn't matter how much time has passed. This is the moment of truth. Don't focus on what you haven't been able to do; just stand in the command of what you're called to do right now. Go do it!

Changes

After dealing with choices and challenges, there may be no way around making changes, but the changes are things that you need to address. There are certain things in your life that you'll need to change to continue on the better road you've chosen. Don't hesitate. Make those changes today.

We can see the example of those who strongly desire to lose weight. Just running out and having gastric bypass surgery isn't the quick fix you might think it is. While the procedure may be fairly simple and quick, you still have to follow changes in your daily life. You may have to change your routine to include exercise. You may need to change your eating habits. You may need to follow up with a psychologist to aid mental wellness as you adjust to relational changes that result from your physical changes. I say all of that to say, while something may seem simple on the surface, there may be follow up steps you aren't aware of. The same is true in this condition.

As I've stated many times before, ultimately, our position is a result of our choices. Therefore, it stands to reason that if you want to change your position, change your choices. It seems simple, doesn't it? Actually, it is. Now, you're thinking, "But wait! You don't understand how enormous my situation is!" You're right; I don't. But I do know that this principle works on every level.

Change–One Step at a Time

The compass slogan of Brian Anderson-Payne Ministries is simply this: "Don't complain about a world that *YOU* won't attempt to change!"While I'm not quick to say things I believe God said to me, I know He said that to me! I've tried to live by that slogan for years now. I'm a big proponent of change. In my inner core, I believe that we can change anything, no matter how big it is. Now, that doesn't mean we can change everything overnight. That might be a stretch. However, anything can change–any ideology, any belief system, any routine, any habit, no matter how long you've had it. There's a saying I often use when I think I'm viewing something improperly. "The only thing I need to do in this situation is to tilt my head." The idea is that tilting my head allows me to view the situation differently, and sometimes, that's all that's necessary to change my perspective on something. If you're thinking that emotions, feelings, or your perceptions on something cannot change, you simply need to tilt your head and get a new perspective.

You can handle any trial, no matter how enormous it is. How do you eat an elephant? One bite at a time. No, you probably can't ingest the entire mammal in one setting, but if you break it down in size, what was impossible becomes possible. It may take some time, but the point is that it will get done. I believe that's the answer to how we accomplish the enormous changes of our lives: one bite at a time.

It has been said that the way to change your life is to change your day. Sometimes we take a step back and look at gigantic changes we wish to make in our lives, but the size of the change seems to put it out of reach. But if we break that change down to bite sizes, it becomes much more accomplishable.

For instance, if you wake up with an enormous plan of losing one hundred pounds, abiding by a better diet, and watching better programs, that could seem monumental. You might not even know where to begin. You might be intimidated about the next nine months of your life. What will they look like? How are you going to succeed in your plans? That's a pretty large chunk of the elephant to swallow. If you asked me where to start, here's what I might say: "Forget about the next nine months. Let's just deal with the next twenty-four hours! Don't even worry about next week.

Let's determine what to do today. How can you eat better today? How can you get five to ten minutes of exercise in today? Let's control what we look at today. Don't even worry about tomorrow; just focus on today." Now, the next day you wake up, I'll say the same thing. Seven days of doing that and we've completed a week of doing the right things. Four weeks of doing that and we've completed a month of doing the right things. It wasn't nearly as intimidating as you thought it would be, either. I'm telling you, that's the ticket. To change your life, change your day.

Therefore, whatever habits we're trying to clear ourselves from, we just change them for today. Let's deal with tomorrow when we get there. If you're trying to get away from the problem of gossiping, tell that friend, "I can't talk about that today." Don't go into a long discussion about how you're becoming someone new and you have turned over a new leaf. That only sets you up for disappointment should you mess up and pick it up again. Too many disappointments and you could start feeling like there's no sense in trying. We're not planning simply to work harder, but we're going to work smarter as well. Your response to unwelcome invitations is simply this: "I'm sorry, but I'm not doing that today." That doesn't signal to others that you're changing your life. It says you are changing your day. However, you're armed with the knowledge that changing your life begins as you change your day!

5

Admit It!, Quit It! Forget It!

> *I'm not saying that I have this all together, that I have it made. But I am well on my way, reaching out for Christ, who has so wondrously reached out for me. Friends, don't get me wrong: By no means do I count myself an expert in all of this, but I've got my eye on the goal, where God is beckoning us onward–to Jesus.*
>
> *–Philippians 3:12-13 (The Message)*

I've always thought that Paul did one of the most difficult things for anyone to do in verse 12. He realized and stated the fact, "I'm not quite where I want to be yet." Even though he talked about some wonderful things in his past, he acknowledged he wasn't where he wanted to be just yet. I think this is difficult for most people but certainly difficult for those in the religious community. We live in the world of "positive affirmation." Therefore, reality is sometimes difficult for some to acknowledge because the mentality often is: "If things are bad, we'll just 'declare' that all is well." I'm in no way speaking against calling "those things which be not as though they were" (Romans 4:17, KJV). That's what God tells us to do; therefore, it is what we should do. At the same time, I don't think God meant for us to deny the reality of where we are presently. If your nose is running, you have fever, and you're coughing and aching, I'm all for declaring that by His stripes you are healed. But you might witness your healing faster if you take some Theraflu because, baby…you're sick!

Since this book deals with failure not being final, you might have to take a second to acknowledge where your failure is. It might be difficult, but hunt the spot of weakness. Identify *the* weight or *the* sin that so easily besets you (Hebrews 12:1). Find your trigger areas.

You Are Here

I'm admittedly one of the most directionally challenged people you will ever meet. I typically can't find my way anywhere easily. Fortunately, I live in the age of technology. No matter what city I travel to, I'm always sure to take my portable navigation system with me. That little thing is amazing! It tells me where to go, how fast I'm going, and the speed limit for that area.

Whoever came up with that idea is a genius, in my book. No matter where I want to go in the United States, if I have an address, my GPS system can get me there. There's only one catch–it has to be able to connect with the satellite and determine where I am presently. Did you catch that? If there's no signal to determine where I am, the system is useless. My point is this: God has given us all the necessary tools to get us to our destinations, no matter where we come from. But we have to be willing and honest enough to admit where we are presently. If you can't admit where you are, you'll be searching for directions that don't make a bit of sense to you. I can give you excellent directions to get from my old house to my mother's house. But what good will those directions do if you're coming from your house?

Like Paul, you have to be willing to take a cold, hard, honest look at yourself and determine, "I am here." Don't just look at your strengths, but include your weaknesses, bad habits, strong suits, and the whole works.

How Scriptures Won't Work

Until you're able to identify your accurate location, you may find yourself feeling like Scripture isn't working for you like you expected. A verse often used in difficult times is Isaiah 54:17, which states, **No weapon that is formed against [me] shall prosper** (KJV). While it is very comforting to fall back on that passage in difficult places, it would be a challenge to understand how you were fired, seemingly without reason, while standing in faith on the Scripture. It's really necessary to identify where you are now. Were you really fired without reason, or are you now reaping unproductive seeds planted? Sometimes a harvest is delayed but not denied. Understand in situations like these, this is no trick of the enemy or anything like that. It's not God spanking you, either. There is a law that God put into motion, and if He will not violate His law, He's not unjust. What is the law? We reap a harvest on the things we sow. That doesn't mean that someone will do to you what you've done to another. That's not how sowing and reaping work. Sowing and reaping are farming terms. In the spring, farmers go out to plant tomato seeds. At harvest time, they don't gather tomato seeds. They receive fully grown, developed tomatoes. Therefore, when you sow one thing, it comes back developed. When a man sows a sperm cell, he reaps a baby. When a speeder sows over-the-limit, fast driving, he reaps a ticket. When a parent sows destructive, critical words to his or her child, the harvest is an underachieving, under producing child. Or possibly that one receives a distant child who doesn't desire a relationship with him or her at all.

When you receive undesirable results, you have to take a look at the entire picture and ask, "Am I really innocent in all this?" If there's any god to blame, it's the god of self. After all, God did give a command for everything to produce after its own kind (Genesis 1). Remember, you were the farmer.

This in no way suggests that we always get our just rewards. I can't tell you the times I've received results that were far less damaging than my initial actions. To this day, I'm still quick to ask God for "crop failure" when I've planted seeds I know I don't wish to receive a full harvest on. Many times, I'm fortunate enough to receive less. However, if I don't receive less, it's not God's fault nor His unfair judgment. It just means I was a successful farmer!

This isn't meant to be discouraging. In all actuality, I think it's empowering. Once again, it strips us from the victim mentality. It says I'm not a victim of my situation; I'm the creator of it. Now, I think this is a necessary part of the process to full recovery because you're bound to repeat cycles you don't understand. I'm able to free my-self of the "woe is me" syndrome when I have a better understanding of how I got here.

So What Now?

If you're reading and feeling like you'll never be able to have a fresh start because you've sowed millions and millions of seeds you never want to harvest, this section is just for you.

> So let's not allow ourselves to get fatigued doing good. At the right time we will harvest a good crop if we don't give up, or quit.
> –Galatians 6:9 (The Message)

Galatians 6:9 always gave me something to ponder once I began to study Scripture in depth. I always wondered why anyone would have to be encouraged while doing well. I thought if someone needed to be encouraged, it would be the person who had a difficult time, not the one who was doing right. I now understand the only time you have to encourage someone who's doing right is when they're doing right but still not getting right, good, or desired results. After checking the context of the verse, I realized I was on the right track. Verse 9 says to stay encouraged, because verse 7 says we reap what we sow. Therefore, even though I may be living in verse 9 today, I can't simply eradicate the time I spent living in verse 7, sowing all kinds of ungodly things.

It's like a person who spends years of foolish living, spending money recklessly, incurring enormous debt. Now that he's come into a right relationship of proper stewardship in his finances, his money troubles might not go away overnight. It's great that he tithes and gives offerings. However, he can't be disappointed because he tithed on Sunday but still received a disconnect notice on Tuesday. Here's where you have to "be not weary" in doing good. Keep doing the right thing even though you don't feel you're receiving right results. Soon, you will have exhausted the results of the negative seeds planted. If you keep doing what is right, paying your bills on time, and not being foolish with your money, good–or certainly better–results are sure to come eventually!

Quit It

It's time to stop! I may not know what it is that you need to stop, but you do. Whatever is holding up your progress, your productivity, your creativity, your authenticity, you have to stop.

I make it sound really simple, don't I? As tremendously difficult as you find the process to be, the first step is actually pretty simple. You have to decide to stop! Here's the cold, hard truth about it. No matter what it is, no matter how damaging it may be, nothing changes until you make the decision to stop. No amount of Bible bashing, lecturing, or anything else, for that matter, will override your decision–not even God! God is a gentleman, and He is not going to force you to do anything. He will encourage you strongly, but He won't force you. That goes against His original design for mankind. He didn't want little robots, remember? He established us with a will, information, and the power to make a choice.

> *Today I have given you the choice between life and death, between blessings and curses. Now I call on heaven and earth to witness the choice you make. Oh, that you would choose life, so that you and your descendants might live!*
> *–Deuteronomy 30:19 (NLT)*

Stop or Be Stopped

There's a difference in deciding to pull the plug on destructive, bad behavior and having the plug pulled on you! Someone might feel, "Who cares how it happened, as long as it happened!" At certain stages, that can be just exactly how you feel. However, there are others who are at different stages, and they may appreciate this section.

I remember hearing one of my childhood teachers, and I, along with the rest of the audience, was amused at his words. He spoke to an august body of listeners and said, "We have to be careful of how we correct young people. Some of us who are older didn't necessarily mature out of certain desires and proclivities; we just got too old for them!" Thanks, Paul Southerland. He was saying not everyone can claim spiritual, mental, or emotional maturity as the reason some of his or her lifestyle habits changed. Sometimes, the person just couldn't physically keep up! This obviously isn't true in all cases, but I think you get the point. Grandparents or even parents may desire to stay up late with their kids on that special weekend binge movie night, but age takes its toll. Sometimes people want to grab that tasty hot dog and shovel it down their throats on the run, like they did years earlier, but the evidence that time moves on becomes apparent if they should try it. It's not that folks don't sometimes have the desire to do certain things, but sometimes time forces a change.

It's empowering to decide to stop certain behavior versus having that decision made for you. I haven't discovered why it works that way, but it does. Remember your younger years when you had to break up with your girlfriend/boyfriend? Even if both of you knew it was a necessary decision, it often had a different impact on you based on who broke up with whom! If you did the dumping, you often processed it one way, but if you were the one dumped, the horse was a different color. Go figure!

I said all of that to say this: Make sure the decision to stop is yours and on your terms. If you can control the timing, avoid waiting until you're forced into a corner. You'll appreciate the results much more.

Quit It–It Begins with a Decision

In 2005, Ruby and I founded a church in Indiana called SOTECM. That stood for Salt of the Earth Christian Ministries. I loved that little group something fierce. It was small but amazing. I can't believe the things I learned about people, leadership, and life in general in that church. One of the things I'll always cherish was the information that came from the ex-drug addicts who were members. They always shared information about the drug culture with me. I have never been a drug addict, so other than television, they were my source of information. I remember talking to Leslie one day, and she was gently correcting my counseling methods with addicts. Every time I came across an addict, I would jump into rescue mode and start figuring out what would make that one's life better. One day Leslie, who was a freed, former addict, slowed me down. She named a few cases in which I needed to back up and basically do nothing. I would ask, "You mean, I'm to do nothing?" She would reply, "Absolutely nothing." You see, being a former addict, she knew there were times when the abuser wasn't really through with his or her drug love affair. For me to attempt to rescue someone who isn't ready to leave the sinking ship is a waste of time, if not a danger to my own safety. The lesson she taught me was that I can't make anyone want to get better. We can encourage them, but the decision has to be theirs. We can whisk them away and lock them in a room, but that's not rescuing them. Once they are able to go free, guess where they're going? You've got it! Straight back to the drug. You want to know the only thing that can get a person off drugs? I'll tell you. It's that person's decision to get off drugs. Anything else is a gamble at best, a waste of time at worst.

Nothing else actually does it. All the jail time in the world won't, in itself, fix the problem. Many people go to jail as addicts, serve several years behind bars, complete their sentences, and go right back to the drugs. Remember, restricted doesn't mean rescued.

Caught Doesn't Mean Completed/Finished

One of the problems of our penal system is thinking that punishment will equate to restoration. That's seldom the case. I write that because many of you reading this book now are acutely aware of your personal failures. Some of them were secret failures, and some were public fiascos. Sometimes, during the initial blast or blowup of a personal failure, we have a myriad of emotions, one of which is guilt. "How could I allow myself to do such a thing?" Great question to ask. However, I encourage you to take the time to really dissect the issue and not just examine the effects of it. Why? Because many times when a personal failure goes public, you're so overwhelmed with popular public disappointment that you rush to position yourself in the proper posture. But rushing to reposition yourself doesn't mean you've clearly disconnected yourself from the true issue at hand. To put it plainly, be careful. Just because your failure has been exposed, that doesn't mean you've made a decision to stop!

Following the reluctant admittance of my affair to my wife, we had a great deal of "intense fellowship" going on that night. All kinds of less than flattering words were thrown around. Actually, my wife was throwing, and I was catching. The levels of guilt, pain, and shame that I felt seemed almost immeasurable. I'm sure it paled in comparison to the pain she was feeling. I remember thinking, *Oh, I wish I could just die right now! If I survive this night, I'll never do something so stupid again!* I immediately took steps to reposition myself, to get away from anything that could possibly remind me of the heartfelt affair that had almost ripped my house, ministry, and life apart. In retrospect, I understand there are sometimes two endings to destructive behavior gone public. The first ending is typically when you're caught. The second ending is once you make a decision to stop the behavior! Both endings may take place simultaneously. At other and more difficult times, the two don't happen contemporaneously. This is the case when something you would rather keep secret has gone public, but you've not yet discovered or developed the strength to let it go. This can cause quite a quandary. At that point, you have the revelation of bad decisions, the disappointment of public opinion, and the addictive, destructive behavior.

> *Consequences don't impede wrong behavior;*
> *they only inspire more creativity.*
> *–Brian Anderson-Payne*

In more than a few cases, failures, bad choices, or wrong decisions have gone public. In itself, this does not stop one from the behavior. I'll go further and say that consequences alone don't stop people from doing wrong things. If a person wants to do something wrong, consequences only make an offender spend more time contemplating how not to get caught. The Old Testament is a striking proof of this. It's full of laws, rules, and regulations for God's people. Even with all those rules, people still continued to miss the mark. The New Testament, however, is full of a different method for reaching the same goal.

The rules and regulations allowed folks at least to understand where they were off, if by chance they didn't already know. In a very small sense, that could be an example of getting caught. It may not bring a great deal of comfort to those like me, who experienced having our failures blasted before folks, but it gives us some sense of community with others.

The Blessing of Being Caught

Some may disagree with me, but I think there are benefits in being caught, however you experience it. You have to learn to look at your glass as half-full and not half-empty. As we speak about making decisions to stop bad behavior, while getting caught won't force that, it may inspire some much needed assistance.

I think there are two groups of people: caught and "uncaught." Those who have been caught should view things differently. There should be passion and compassion not always found in those who have not yet been caught. First, understand that there are many ways of getting caught. It doesn't always mean what you may think. You can be caught by personal conviction, as was the Bible's prodigal son in Luke 15:17-19. Or you can experience public arrest like the woman caught in adultery in John 8:3. We will discuss her shortly.

If you've been privately caught, you have time to assess your situation, eradicate bad behavior, and rearrange your steps or "come to yourself" before your shortcomings or issues are discovered by others. The publicly caught don't have that liberty. They still have to assess and correct their behavior and rearrange their steps, but because their misstep is known by others, they have to do this under the watchful and sometimes judgmental eye of other imperfect people.

Whichever group you are a part of, this information

will be helpful. However, in this section I want to address those of you who have been publicly caught. I realize that you battle not only the pain of your offense but also the weight of public speculation. You are not the first, you won't be the last, but you can be one of the successful overcomers.

> *The teachers of the law and the Pharisees brought in a woman caught in adultery. They made her stand before the group and said to Jesus, "Teacher, this woman was caught in the act of adultery. In the Law Moses commanded us to stone such women. Now what do you say?" They were using this question as a trap, in order to have a basis for accusing him. But Jesus bent down and started to write on the ground with his finger. When they kept on questioning him, he straightened up and said to them, "If any one of you is without sin, let him be the first to throw a stone at her." Again he stooped down and wrote on the ground. At this, those who heard began to go away one at a time, the older ones first, until only Jesus was left, with the woman still standing there. Jesus straightened up and asked her, "Woman, where are they? Has no one condemned you?" "No one, sir," she said. "Then neither do I condemn you," Jesus declared. "Go now and leave your life of sin."*
> *–John 8:3-11*

I wanted to discuss this woman to bring some sense of comfort to all of those who don't seem to be able to recover from the shame, not of making bad choices but of having those bad choices put on blast! That's how this woman had to feel. It would be pretty hard to beat the embarrassment she felt. It's certainly one thing to admit to your discrepancies, but to be discovered in the middle of them? The story doesn't tell us her opinion of adultery. When the account is first presented, we don't know if she loved what she did or if she hated it. That's the problem with being publicly caught. All people know is what you did. They seldom consider how you feel about it. Sometimes, you hate what you're doing more than those do who found you doing it! Obviously, this woman was in the position of hating what she did also. Why? Because when Jesus gave her a way out, she took it! As I stated earlier, it doesn't matter who swoops in as your knight in shining armor. If you're not ready to be rescued, no one can do anything for you.

Now, here's the best part. According to Scripture, this woman had done something worthy of death. By public opinion, she was about to die! Jesus came to this woman's defense and set her free of the charges placed on her. He also gave her a warning not to find herself in this predicament again; He might not be there to get her out of trouble the next time. Now, picture this woman walking around town. You can just hear the whispers: "You know that's Mrs. Adultery right there! Somebody ought to do something about her." Let's imagine her response. "Oh, I'm sorry to inform you, but I've already come up on charges for that! I was accused and guilty as charged, but Jesus set me free. So you'll have to find something else on me if you're expecting me to live in guilt and shame! I've been set free from my mistakes. No more holding my head down when I walk through town. So now, not only do you know what I did, but you know what I survived. Have a great day!"

Typically, when I hear sermons on this passage of Scripture, people bring up the fact that the man wasn't brought before the crowd. I'll bet at that moment the man was celebrating, feeling that he had gotten out of that mess because he didn't get caught. However, just think about it. That woman getting caught could have been the best thing that ever happened to her. She was forced to face her issue, and she was given a second chance. So many people are never forced to uncover their issue. Therefore, it hides in the crevices of their life, slowly snatching pieces continually. However, when you have been forced to consider issues for what they are, they very likely begin to lose power in your life. What is it that secretly dwells in your life and allows you to have a false sense of goodness when you look at others? In your own way, pull the cover off that area to deal with it face to face. Take back your power. Then you, too, can tell the accuser, "My issues have been faced and handled. Jesus has already dealt with me on that one. He's over it, and so am I!"

Don't be afraid to address it honestly. Remember, He is waiting to present you with His mercy. Mercy presupposes guilt. If you can't admit your guilt, you cannot receive His mercy. Once you realize you have His mercy, you can stand in His grace to leave it all behind you.

Remember to Forget

By now, you're aware that certain themes, thoughts, and ideas are simply being repeated in different formats. That's a powerful and proven formula. It's true what they say, "Repetition is the best teacher." With that being said, I won't take time here to re-illustrate my understanding of the apostle Paul's idea concerning Philippians 3:13. I explained myself pretty thoroughly in chapter 3.

Here, I'll just suggest the significance of actively pursuing forgetting. There's a reason I titled this section, "Remember to Forget." Typically, we don't put much thought into the things we forget. Honestly, we seldom set out to forget things. How often did you mean to forget something important like your phone number? It's not your plan to forget your loved one's birthday. Those things generally happen by mistake. Because of that, we seldom consider purposely trying to forget something; we generally don't practice forgetting.

No doubt, we'd love to forget the painful or embarrassing experiences of life. Those things we'd like to forget often have a way of attaching themselves to our conscious minds. Without a medical malfunction, forget-ting doesn't come naturally. We have to work at moving beyond certain experiences. They can't be removed from our memory banks, but they can be conquered or overcome. A person who experiences a painful divorce probably won't be able to forget that event. Certain memories will probably continue to pop up periodically. But one can go through the process of being able to get beyond it and have healthy post-divorce relationships. That's the whole point of forgetting. It isn't not being aware of certain experiences. It's just being able to function productively in spite of them. That doesn't mean you operate in anger or bitterness about what happened, either. It does not mean that you pretend to have moved on when, in actuality, you carry secret pain about it in every waking thought. It means you actually find some sense of peace and tranquility over the entire matter. If you got fired from a job and sometime later you see that boss and feel a need to let him know that you made it anyway, you haven't moved on yet. You still believe you have something to prove. If someone hurt you and you still feel the need to let her see your progress, you haven't been freed totally from that situation yet. When you are truly free, you'll know it! There will be nothing to prove and no need to prove it! Life has moved on. You are now setting out to forget some things.

That should be our goal. Find everything that hurts, that slows you down, and that distracts you, and remember to forget. Make it a goal to find the spot where you can think on the person, place, or thing and feel no debilitating, paralyzing weights. In short, forget it!

6

You Can Begin Again

Forget the former things; do not dwell on the past. See, I am doing a new thing!
–Isaiah 43:18-19

I titled this chapter, "You Can Begin Again," with the hope of leaving that simple yet profound thought heavy in your head and on your heart. It's a straightforward thought. It's a weighty thought, yet many times it is a difficult idea to be convinced of. You literally can begin again. No matter what area of life you're dealing with, starting over commences with a decision to do so. Now, I'm not saying that is all it entails, but it certainly begins there. All the other tools we'll discuss throughout the rest of this chapter will render themselves useless without an initial, firm decision to start again!

A "Do Over"

Amid the chaos of my childhood, I also have some pretty wonderful and vivid memories. I grew up in and around church. At the age of ten, I was already holding a leadership position with the Universal Church of Truth youth department in Indianapolis, Indiana. Our church was a family-based church, and most folks were pretty well connected. The adults spent a lot of time together, so that allowed us children to do the same. On Sunday afternoons, we would all follow our pastor (who's also my uncle) two blocks down the street to "Mama Van's" house for the greatest macaroni and cheese you've ever tasted! Mama Van is present with the Lord now, but if the angels know like I know, I'm sure they have her standing at that stove in the sky even now! Anyway, as protocol would have it, all the kids would have to play outside until dinner was ready. The other few boys and I mostly would watch the girls play. I hold very clear memories of watching Monica, Valerie, Sherry, Terry, and the other girls play a game called Jacks. With one hand, a player would bounce a tiny ball and swoop up as many game pieces as possible before the ball bounced again. Every now and then, the pieces would be spaced too far apart to be picked up. Occasionally, rather than try and certainly fail, the player would just yell out, "Do over!" That would allow her an opportunity to start over. The concept is totally encouraging! Wouldn't it be wonderful on those days we wake up on the wrong side of the bed just to yell, "Do over"? Or what about a five second grace period after saying the wrong thing to yell, "Do over"? If that were possible, many people would still have their old jobs, old friends, and so on! Maybe none of us can call for that, but we can start again.

Starting Again versus Quitting

This writing in no way encourages a quitting or a give-up mentality. While starting over and quitting might look similar at times, there's a great difference between the two. Quitting or giving up accepts and surrenders to the inevitability of failure. Starting again accepts and surrenders to the inevitability of success. It says, "The last attempt didn't accomplish the goal, but the next one will!" Starting again is pursuing the same goal using different methods and measures. Starting again says succeeding is too significant to let past failures to hinder it!

What makes a person decide to start over? When thinking about this chapter, I wrote a new quote.

New beginnings happen where old ones fail!
–Brian Anderson-Payne

When something in you looks at the failure of yesterday but refuses to accept it as law, the stage is set for a new beginning. I'm not sure there are many more options. You can wallow in regrets, or you can chart a new course. This seems to operate in stages.

Often, when you arrive at a destination other than the one you aimed for, there's a time of reflection and observation. What happens next is most important. How do you handle the disappointment of missed goals? Those moments determine greatness. We all fall, but we don't all choose to recover.

Fall seven times, stand up eight.
–Japanese proverb

Here's the point. Everyone can begin again! It really doesn't matter how old or young you are. It doesn't matter how rich or poor you are. It doesn't matter how intelligent or illiterate you are. It does not matter if you are established or a novice. It doesn't matter if you've been doing things for fifty years or if you're just in the planning stages. It doesn't matter if you have a perfect track record or no track record. If you want to, if you choose to, if you decide to, you can begin again!

Presenting my next subject requires a great amount of skill and tact. I'm not convinced that I possess the proper amount of either for such a weighty subject, but I trust the insight that says there's safety in the multitude of counsel. In other words, several of my peers, mentors, and teachers will check my words. If that isn't enough, I trust the guidance of the Holy Spirit. Okay, here we go!

Even God Began Again!

The LORD was grieved that He had made man on the earth, and His heart was filled with pain. So the LORD said, "I will wipe mankind, whom I have created, from the face of the earth–men and animals, and creatures that move along the ground, and birds of the air–for I am grieved that I have made them." But Noah found favor in the eyes of the LORD.
–Genesis 6:6-8

It's a pretty heavy statement to make, saying even God began again! Why would God have to start over? Is it possible for God to make a mistake? Nope, not at all.

Let me begin by explaining that one of the traits that makes God who He is, is the fact that He possesses three characteristics none other possesses: omnipresence, omnipotence, and omniscience. Omnipresence means He's "all present" or that He's everywhere at the same time. Omnipotence says He's "all powerful" or He's sovereign. Omniscience says He's "all knowing," and that's the one we want here. If God is "all knowing"–and I believe He is–that means He possesses all information at all times. He has full knowledge of yesterday, today, and tomorrow. If He's omniscient, He knows everything; therefore, He cannot learn. Learning would mean there is information He doesn't somehow already have. Not possessing any information of any matter would rob Him of His claim to be God. Therefore, nothing can ever catch Him off guard, because He already knows. He gives others the opportunity to make their own decisions, but those decisions are only surprising to those who make them, not to God Himself. Therefore, when the Bible speaks in terms like "God repented" or "God changed His mind," those statements are simply to show us the gravity of the situation. They are what are known as anthropomorphism. That's simply taking a non-human object/entity and describing it in human terms.

It's really not possible for God to change His mind. Changing His mind doesn't fit Him. You and I change our minds because we receive information that we didn't have previously. New information causes us to feel as if we can make better decisions. But what would happen if we never came across new information? What if we already knew all the facts about a situation? Then, there would be no need ever to change our mind because we would never learn anything we didn't already know. That is how things are with God. He doesn't ever need to change His mind because He already holds all information. Therefore, even the concept of Him changing His mind is simply to illustrate how significant a situation is to Him. He allows us to see how heavy a matter weighs on His heart.

So you're wondering: How does the text listed above apply? Either God knew or He didn't know what man was going to do. If He did know (which He did), why would He begin all over again? Obviously, God knew what man would do before man knew. Proof? Sure. Man's sin was eating from the tree of the knowledge of good and evil, right? But there was another extremely significant tree in the garden as well. It was the tree of life, which represented Christ. Why would we have a need for the tree of life when man had not experienced death yet, unless God knew it was only a matter of time? Keep in mind that Revelation 13:8 refers to the Lamb that was slain from (or before) the foundation of the world. Before man had the chance to fall, God had already prepared his restoration process; therefore, man's failure was no real surprise to God.

A Starting-over Example

There is a very simple answer as to why God had to begin again. Most importantly, here is the example our heavenly Father leaves for us. His goal was to have a creation that would be loving and would obediently serve Him by their own free will. When the first design didn't operate on that level, rather than give up, He returned to the drawing board. I believe the picture is more for our edification than anything else. Many of us reading this book are in great pursuit of something. For some of us, we've run into multiple roadblocks and barriers. You certainly have one option (that I don't recommend) to give up, throw in the towel, and call it a day. The other option is to determine that the goal is far too important for you to quit before reaching it. You just have to begin again. You have to look at the vision you began with, identify where you are presently, and determine if you've reached your mark. If the steps of yesterday didn't accomplish the desired goal, you can simply start again.

Only <u>You</u> Can Decide to Begin Again!

Please don't assume that my ease of writing the words "just begin again" will mean the decision to do so will be easy. I'm well aware that it won't be. Sometimes, making that forward-moving decision will be one of the most difficult things to do. I understand that on the heels of a major disappointment, attempting the effort again and running the risk of another disappointment is often the last thing on one's mind! Oh, yes, I know what it feels like to take a blow so painful that I conclude, "Boy, I'll never try that again!" That's why I've written this section. If you've experienced that debilitating kind of hurt, these words are exclusively for you!

The Perfect Environment

No matter how the stage has been set, as it has been echoed throughout this book, the final decision is yours! All that life can do is present the perfect stage or environment for the perfect "do over." Life will set the stage several times for you to begin again. However, it's for you to choose to seize the opportunity or to continue the mundane cycle of comfort.

> *No one else can create your new beginning. They can only create the perfect environment for it to take place!*
> *–Brian Anderson-Payne*

It's my charge now to open your eyes to the multiple opportunities that you've been given on a regular basis to experience the grandness of purpose. I'm not surprised that so many of us often miss the wonderful chances because of the package they so often come in.

Sometimes, our greatest gifts come in the most undesirable packages. You can desire to start your own business. You can do the research for that business. You can even prepare an incredible business plan that comforts and establishes your route to success for the idea. But then you can step back and conclude, "It's not the right time in my life for such a venture." You've decided that because of all the financial responsibilities you have. You just don't think you can afford to chase the dream right now. Going into work the following Monday morning and getting a pink slip may seem like the ultimate nightmare! I would probably feel terrified as well. What a nightmare! But wait. Is it? Is it really a nightmare, or is it an opportunity to begin again? Have you been handed an opportunity to get out there and make that vision come to pass? Right now, you're standing at the moment of truth. Here is where you decide either to jump back into that comfort zone and start beating the pavement, continuing the mundane path of the past, or to seize the opportunity for your new beginning. Remember, **no one else can create your new beginning. They can only create the perfect environment for it to take place!**

The loss of a marriage or a friendship, the death of a dream will not automatically create a new beginning for you. Yet it serves as a platform for you to create one!

Well, if my vote counts for anything (and the mere fact that you're reading my book says it does), I say, "Don't dare get back in that box!" Take a deep breath, square your shoulders, and snatch your new beginning.

New Beginnings Have Great Cost; Maintaining Old Ones Cost Even More!

Resolving to start again is costly. It's often difficult. You will have to battle all kinds of mental and emotional demons. You'll have to convince yourself that moving forward is worth all the hard work it entails. In short, a new beginning has a great cost, but many times, maintaining the old, failed past could cost you even more than starting over.

> One day Sarah saw the son that Hagar the Egyptian had borne to Abraham, poking fun at her son Isaac. She told Abraham, "Get rid of this slave woman and her son. No child of this slave is going to share inheritance with my son Isaac!" The matter gave great pain to Abraham–after all, Ishmael was his son. But God spoke to Abraham, "Don't feel badly about the boy and your maid. Do whatever Sarah tells you. Your descendants will come through Isaac. Regarding your maid's son, be assured that I'll also develop a great nation from him–he's your son, too."
>
> –Genesis 21:9-13 (The Message)

> Some of us think holding on makes us strong; but sometimes it is letting go.
>
> –Herman Hesse

Every new beginning comes from some other beginning's end.
                                        –Seneca

Courage is the power to let go of the familiar.
                                        –Raymond Lindquist

Discontent is the first necessity of progress.
                                        –Thomas Edison

Here's what may be considered a difficult yet truthful fact: Tomorrow won't share with yesterday. You have to choose who gets your attention!

The fact of the matter is simply this: For some, a new beginning should not feel like an option. It's something you have to do. You can't keep going in circles. Refusing to make a fresh start is costing you energy, time, vision, passion, and drive. When you've been given the grace to move forward and choose not to, the conflict of such a choice begins to show. Allow me to illustrate this point. When a working relationship has run its course and both parties know it but refuse to address it, not doing so will only allow more tension to develop. You may notice that you bump heads more often. Even the smallest things potentially can begin to seem enormous. Why? Because when it's time for a new beginning, avoiding that step will simply add more pressure on the old system. Maybe the case isn't that you discontinue your relationship, but you may need to address certain issues that happened but have been avoided. At any rate, the old procedure is no longer working, and it's time for a new beginning!

7

Restoration-God's Idea, God's Example

Support can be given from a distance, but restoration requires a hands-on approach. You can't restore what you won't touch!
-Brian Anderson-Payne

Restoration. It is such a wonderful word to hear. In certain environments, it's thrown around quite a bit. However, the use of the word doesn't always guarantee the demonstration of the word. To demonstrate restoration is a bit of work. It doesn't happen by mistake. If a healthy restoration of another is the goal, you won't be able to accomplish it without thought and real consideration. Before we delve into it, let's first get an understanding of what the word "restoration" means.

Merriam Webster Online definition of *restoration:*
1: an act of restoring or the condition of being restored: as a: bringing back to a former position or condition: REINSTATEMENT <the restoration of peace> b: RESTITU-TION c: a restoring to an unimpaired or improved condition <the *restoration* of a painting>
2: something that is restored; especially a representation or reconstruction of the original form (as of a fossil or a building).

Yourdictionary.com online definition of *restoration:*
1. A restoring or being restored; specif., a. Reinstatement in a former position, rank, etc. b. Restitution for loss, damage, etc. c. a putting or bringing back into a former, normal, or unimpaired state or condition
2. A representation or reconstruction of the original form or structure, as of a building, fossil, animal, etc.
3. Something restored.

Dictionary.com definition of *restoration:*
1. The act of restoring; renewal, revival, or reestablishment.
2. The state or fact of being restored.
3. A return of something to a former, original, normal, or unimpaired condition.
4. Restitution of something taken away or lost.
5. Something that is restored, as by renovating.
6. A reconstruction or reproduction of an ancient building, extinct animal, or the like, showing it in its original state.
7. A putting back into a former position, dignity, etc.
8. *Dentistry.*

a. the work, process, or result of replacing or restoring teeth or parts of teeth.

b. something that restores or replaces teeth or parts of teeth, as a filling, crown, or denture.

9. The Restoration,

a. the reestablishment of the monarchy in England with the return of Charles II in 1660.

b. the period of the reign of Charles II (1660-85), sometimes extended to include the reign of James II (1685-88).

I listed several definitions of "restoration." Did you notice a recurring theme? It's all about bringing a thing back to its former state. It's about making something proper again. The idea is that whatever broken or lesser condition a person, place, or thing finds itself in, the process of restoration can and should undo the effects of the mishap. That's a powerful thought! If something can be created wonderfully, experience a shape-shifting negative experience, but then undergo restoration to its former (and better) state, what power does the negative experience possess any longer? With that train of thought, I can see why God would give such a powerful tool to people who are commanded to love each other.

I believe the gift of restoration is to help each of us navigate through life. Perhaps, it would be wonderful if in this life we never encountered obstacles, setbacks, trip ups, or mistakes. However, that's not the case. In life, we often find ourselves up against all kinds of debilitating situations and circumstances. Many times our mistakes or the images thereof sneak themselves into the crevices of our minds and hearts and make progress or forward motion quite difficult. But for those of us who have been the recipient of true restoration, the mistakes of the past don't hold the same power that they may hold over another. Our job is to see that everybody receives it! Restoration is the tool that allows us to turn yesterday's mistakes into tomorrow's motivation.

A central point to understand is that restoration is not a human idea. It is God's idea. He was the first to implement and demonstrate it. Therefore, restoration is not just something that the Almighty hoped we humans would think of kindly enough to embrace. He displayed it first, to give us a proper way to view it and an understanding of how to use it. As we look at scriptural text concerning it, there's much for us to take away.

The overall idea of restoration is putting something back into its proper position or corrected state. The following texts show something very interesting concerning God's thoughts of practice of restoration.

The saving work of Christ was understood and spiritually demonstrated before the world was physically created. Romans 5:12 teaches that sin entered the world through the disobedience of Adam, who ate from the tree of the knowledge of good and evil, thereby creating a need for the restoration of mankind. Yet God's presentation of His restorative process seems to have been implemented long before it was ever needed.

> *Therefore, just as sin entered the world through one man, and death through sin, and in this way death came to all men, because all sinned.*
>
> *–Romans 5:12*

I hope my listing the following verses of Scripture helps you to see that God was well at work on the restoration process long before man had even fallen. Wow! What a proactive God we trust in!

> *When the woman saw that the fruit of the tree was good for food and pleasing to the eye, and also desirable for gaining wisdom, she took some and ate it. She also gave some to her husband, who was with her, and he ate it. Then the eyes of both of them were opened, and they realized they were naked; so they sewed fig leaves together and made coverings for themselves.*
>
> *–Genesis 3:6-7*

> *For you know that it was not with perishable things such as silver and gold that you were redeemed from the empty way of life handed down to you from your forefathers, but with the precious blood of Christ, a lamb without blemish or defect. **He was chosen before the creation of the world, but was revealed in these last times for your sake.** Through him you believe in God, who raised him from the dead and glorified him, and so your faith and hope are in God.*
>
> *–I Peter 1:18-21 (Emphasis mine)*

Praise be to the God and Father of our Lord Jesus Christ, who has blessed us in the heavenly realms with every spiritual blessing in Christ. **For he chose us in him before the creation of the world to be holy and blameless in his sight.** *In love he predestined us to be adopted as his sons through Jesus Christ, in accordance with his pleasure and will.*
–Ephesians 1:3-5 (Emphasis mine)

Who has saved us and called us to a holy life– not because of anything we have done but because of his own purpose and grace. **This grace was given us in Christ Jesus before the beginning of time,** *but it has now been revealed through the appearing of our Savior, Christ Jesus, who has destroyed death and has brought life and immortality to light through the gospel.*
–II Timothy 1:9-10 (Emphasis mine)

And we know that in all things God works for the good of those who love him, who have been called according to his purpose. **For those God fore-knew he also predestined to be conformed to the likeness of his Son, that he might be the firstborn among many brothers.** *And those he predestined, he also called; those he called, he also justified; those he justified, he also glorified.*
–Romans 8:28-30 (Emphasis mine)

Proactive, Not Reactive

Following God's example, restoration is indeed proactive. Based on the mere concept of restoration, it may be difficult to see it as proactive versus reactive. After all, the concept is to put something or someone back in its proper state. That suggests you can't restore someone until they've at least been removed from their proper or initial state. That idea causes us to see restoration as reactive. It appears to react to a fall or error of some type. Yet when we look at the example God gave us, His preparation of restoration was before man's fall while His implementation was after man's fall. In other words, although He may not have been able to implement it yet, He was certainly prepared with restoration.

This teaches us that we have to consider the steps of restoration long before they are needed. In the area of friendship, disappointment comes from not anticipating it or thinking it's even possible. "How could you lie to me?" is the question we ask when betrayed by a close friend. "How could you two get a divorce after all these years?" "How could you steal from someone?" "How could you. . . ?" Sometimes, the mere shock, horror, or surprise suggests that we never dreamed disappointment was possible. I'm not suggesting we go around thinking the worst about people, but if Scripture is true and mankind has a weakness through flesh (Romans 8:3), we have to understand that, unfortunately, anything really is possible. Expect the best; fore think the worst. A parent is absolutely devastated when a teenage daughter comes home pregnant. Few of you reading this would look forward to such a situation. I'm not suggesting you should, either. I know I wouldn't want to deal with it. However, if we are unable even to consider such possibilities, how can we ever expect to handle negative experiences outside the mere assistance of luck? Fore-thinking such situations doesn't necessarily make them easier to deal with, but it potentially can remove a bit of the anxiety from your life. Some people avoid such things for fear that thinking on something is "calling things that be not" into existence. I have to disagree. You're not expecting or desiring situations. You're thinking, "Just like I have sometimes surprised myself in life, it's possible that someone else could surprise me, too!" This thought process is simply a fire extinguisher. Millions of folks live in homes where they walk by fire extinguishers every day that they do not consciously consider. They don't recognize them because they don't think about them. They hope never to need them. I hope you never need them, either! However, should a day arise when you need them, I sure hope you have them!

Understanding that restoration is proactive, let's consider methods of implementing it before it is necessary. If you were preparing for a big holiday meal, you probably wouldn't wait until your guests arrived to consider what to purchase at the market. If you know guests are coming, wisdom will encourage you to prepare early. Friends, mistakes of those we are connected to are coming. Wisdom encourages us to prepare early.

The Purpose of Restoration–To Fix
What Has Been Broken

Indeed, restoration is here to undo the effects of that which has gone wrong. Succinctly, it is to fix what was broken. If the question is, "Who needs restoration?" the answer is, "The one who ceases to operate (due to misfortune) as he or she was designed to." Never allow restoration to be hindered from those areas where God desires it most. Some misunderstand God's corrective measures. No doubt, He is not opposed to brokenness. Indeed, there are verses of Scripture that give us a picture of His attitude concerning brokenness.

> *The sacrifices of God are a broken spirit; a broken and contrite heart, O God, you will not despise.*
> *–Psalm 51:17*

The words of David following his sin with Bathsheba express his emotion and conversation with God. God is not bothered by brokenness, which is simply to have godly sorrow. A broken spirit is one that is truly repentant and aware of its great need for God. This is an emotion that does not sadden God but rather pleases Him on some level. However, God does not take joy when His children are "crippled." There is a difference in being broken and being crippled. Even in medical science, when a bone has been fractured and is not growing properly, a doctor may reset the bone. This merely means the bone is broken and placed in the proper position to grow back healthy and stronger. The intended result is an even stronger bone. The bone will perhaps develop with more stability than it had before the initial break or injury. Without being told, you may never know the damaged condition the bone was once in. However, being crippled is another story. An individual who has been crippled is a very apparent ordeal. He is changed and compromised after the crippling event. While crippled, he is not able to perform at greater levels than before the incident. This is a case where outside restoration is necessary. Notice the story of the prodigal son.

> *Jesus continued: "There was a man who had two sons. The younger one said to his father, 'Father, give me my share of the estate.' So he divided his property between them. Not long after that, the younger son got together all he had, set off for a distant country and there squandered his wealth in wild living. After he had spent everything, there was a severe famine in that whole country, and he began to be in need. So he went and hired himself out to a citizen of that country, who sent him to his fields to feed pigs.He longed to fill his stomach with the pods that the pigs were eating, but no one gave him anything. When he came to his senses, he said, 'How many of my father's hired men have food to spare, and here I am starving to death!' "*
> *–Luke 15:11-17*

Up to this point, it appears that we're just seeing an attitude that I imagine is all too familiar in many of the families of those reading this book. A young person has taken the attitude of entitlement too far and has gone out, lived wild and recklessly, fell on hard times, had the revelation thereof, and decided to go home financially ruined, humiliated, embarrassed, and totally humbled. There's nothing too foreign here. As a matter of fact, I've heard this text preached many times. Typically, when I have heard it preached, the second state of the young man seems almost something to be glorified. They speak of how he was humbled and brought low. A preacher will yell, "You know, God knows how to bring you down a notch! You can't get too high!" I'm not sure I agree with their assessment of the situation. On second glance at the story, I don't think the young man's state was something to be envied at all. In actuality, this young man was pushed far beyond the point of being humbled to the place of being crippled.

> *I will set out and go back to my father and say to him: Father, I have sinned against heaven and against you. I am no longer worthy to be called your son; make me like one of your hired men.*
> *–Luke 15:18-19*

This almost looks admirable on the surface, doesn't it? The son finally realized the error of his ways, yet–though he sinned against heaven and his father–the image he now has of himself is wrong. Notice his words, "I am no longer worthy to be called your son." Based on the foolish decisions he had made, he had changed the view he had of his true position. It would be possible for us to think that he was correct in his view of self if we didn't have the father's opinion of the situation.

> *So he got up and went to his father. "But*
> *while he was still a long way off, his father*
> *saw him and was filled with compassion for*
> *him; he ran to his son, threw his arms around*
> *him and kissed him. "The son said to him,*
> *'Father, I have sinned against heaven and*
> *against you. I am no longer worthy to be*
> *called your son. But the father said to his*
> *servants, 'Quick! Bring the best robe and put*
> *it on him. Put a ring on his finger and sandals*
> *on his feet. Bring the fattened calf and kill it.*
> *Let's have a feast and celebrate. For this son*
> *of mine was dead and is alive again; he was*
> *lost and is found.' So they began to celebrate.*
> –Luke 15:20-24

I know, because of the father's reaction, that the son had an incorrect view of himself. Before the son could complete all the things he had purposed to say to his father once he reached him, the father cut him off. As a matter of fact, before the son could say anything, he was overwhelmed with a display of affection from a joyful, loving father. When the son said, "I don't deserve even the title of your son," the father's actions said, "Let me show you just how wrong you are! Not only will I still call you son, but I'll also demonstrate the privileges of a son over a servant." The father said not to give his son "things" but the "best of things." The father demanded that they erase all traces of his past. The servants were instructed to make him look like his true person! Finally, they were to prepare an atmosphere of celebration for others to participate in as well.

Notice the steps here. First, the father initiated the

direction by lavishing the son with kisses and hugs. He made it clear that he was genuinely excited about his son's return. He did not take this initial meeting to inform the son of his foolish decisions. There would be opportunities for that later. However, this was not the time for rebuke or chastisement. This was a very delicate moment in the life of his son, who apparently was already on the edge.

Second, the father demonstrated his heart while simultaneously combating the son's thoughts of unworthiness. The adorning of his son was much more than just some physical or outward display. Words of affirmation are wonderful, but sometimes words must be upstaged by actions. In one who wrestles with unworthiness, his demeanor will not appear as strong as it has in the past. This is the evidence that one has been crippled. He now walks with a limp, whereas in times past he didn't. His attitude is less than joyful, whereas it once was radiant. His speech is without great impact, whereas at one time it held much.

Third, the father called for a celebration with other guests. It was no small event he announced to everyone as cause for the celebration; it was the return of his son! The significance here is the fact that an atmosphere of celebration for the lost son was being set. While the father was out to accomplish restoration, he entreated with others to play a part as well. As I've stated earlier, environments are significant to restoration as they are significant to destruction. Certain environments are conducive for restoration.

Likewise, some environments must be avoided during times of healing. Depending on the level of public awareness of your mishap, you may need to avoid certain places or people until you're healed enough to be there. How can you know if it's a good place to be or not? If the environment is not willing to celebrate you in spite of your bad decisions, it's not the best place to be right now. Avoid places that can only celebrate you based on the level of your performance. Everyone who is in the father's house in the parable was there to celebrate the return of his son.

Just so I don't leave you in the dark, I want you to understand that there is another attitude lingering close in the dark places outside the party.

> Meanwhile, the older son was in the field. Then he came near the house, he heard music and dancing. So he called one of the servants and asked him what was going on. "Your brother has come," he replied, "and your father has killed the fattened calf because he has him back safe and sound." The older brother became angry and refused to go in.
> –Luke 15:25-28

The Problem of Restoration

Don't be fooled. Not everyone will come to your party. Not everyone wants to celebrate you, and you're going to have to deal with that. Understand that when I say, "You have to deal with that," I mean you have to be aware of it. I don't mean you have to place yourself in that environment. You may have to be around people who aren't out to restore you, but you don't have to seek them out! Watch where you place yourself right now. Watch whom you give an ear to. It may not be good to read every article you see online at this time. Some things might just keep you feeling guilty or shameful.

We have to be real and to admit that some aren't going to celebrate you because of how it makes them feel about themselves. The problem with the sin nature is that it always places self above others. As distorted as the view is, some still believe that the image of another has to be down before the image of themselves can be up. But here is the solid truth about it: Holding you down doesn't lift me up! Actually, it works the opposite. Visualize the image. If you're trying to reach the top of a ladder and your focus is more on holding the next person down, you can't be doing a great job of climbing. That's the problem with attempting to hold others back.

Just as some appear to be committed to keeping you from restoration, others are committed to making sure you receive it!

The older brother became angry and refused to go in. So his father went out and pleaded with him. But he answered his father, "Look! All these years I've been slaving for you and never disobeyed your orders. Yet you never gave me even a young goat so I could celebrate with my friends. But when this son of yours who has squandered your property with prostitutes comes home, you kill the fattened calf for him!" "My son," the father said, "you are always with me, and everything I have is yours. But we had to celebrate and be glad, because this brother of yours was dead and is alive again; he was lost and is found."

–Luke 15:28-32

Notice how the son refused to go in! He couldn't go in because the house was filled with celebration. Those who refuse to restore will avoid atmospheres set on doing so. Yet notice the attitude of the restorer. The father went outside as well. He wouldn't stand for less than a celebrant's attitude inside, but he would also attempt to change the minds of others outside. There's a picture of a father, pleading, "I want you inside, celebrating your brother, but I won't have you inside destroying him."

Unfortunately, man is often at war with himself. He battles that fleshly part of himself that resists preferring "another above himself." When he has done so, he will admit that restoration is fully attainable. We have to free ourselves from what I call "stinking thinking." Occasionally, we've been inundated with wrong information or ideas that lead us down incorrect corridors of thought.

Hearing Fairytales

In 1803, *Mother Goose's Melody* was published. Inside the collection of stories was the famous nursery rhyme, "Humpty Dumpty." The modern version reads:

Humpty Dumpty sat on a wall;
Humpty Dumpty had a great fall.
All the king's horses and all the king's men
Couldn't put Humpty together again.

I realize the story is just a fairytale, and far be it from me to tell someone what to spread or not spread. But for me, my thoughts have changed. While it didn't take me long to memorize the story as a child, I have a different idea as an adult. You can quote me. "If the king's horses and the king's men couldn't put Humpty Dumpty back together again, he was living in the wrong kingdom." You and I are commanded to "put people back together again." That's our job! That's what restoration is. I have chosen not to leave others with the idea that they just have to deal with the rest of their lives as broken pieces. You can be put back together again! (I think you have to check any emotions that leave you wanting to leave others broken.)

What to Do Now?

Jesus went through all the towns and villages, teaching in their synagogues, preaching the good news of the kingdom and healing every disease and sickness. When he saw the crowds, he had compassion on them, because they were harassed and helpless, like sheep without a shepherd. Then he said to the disciples, "The harvest is plentiful but the workers are few. Ask the Lord of the harvest, therefore, to send out workers into his harvest field."

–Matthew 9:35-38

There is much to be done, no matter what side of the fence you're on. We, like Jesus, need the burden of seeing more concerned folks to show up on the scene. Some need to be receiving the restorative power of love and getting back up and into the game. Others need to be actively pursuing those who need to receive that love. I want to throw a few points at you before closing this book and commissioning you to get to work.

Point one: You can support from a distance, but restoration requires hands on!

We are aware of what love is because the qualities are listed in I Corinthians 13:4-7. It's very possible to have great love for a person with whom you don't have constant or regular contact with. Imagine the parents or relatives who love others through all types of situations. You can love someone with whom you're disappointed. Just because you don't talk on a regular basis doesn't mean there's a lack of love. The fact that you don't see each other on a consistent basis expresses no disdain or lack of love. You can stand in someone's corner even if you haven't spoken in quite some time. However, to restore someone, you will have to remove that distance.

Restoration can't be done from a distance. It requires hands-on activity. It can't be done in silence. Waiting in the wings for one to recover can't be seen as restoration. It may be patiently supporting him, but it is not restoring him. You will definitely have to make that occasional call just to check up on him or to speak life to him.

Point two: Restoration isn't based on the ability of the wounded.

> When Mephibosheth son of Jonathan, the son of Saul, came to David, he bowed down to pay him honor. David said, "Mephibosheth!" "Your servant," he replied. "Don't be afraid," David said to him, "for I will surely show you kindness for the sake of your father Jonathan. I will restore to you all the land that belonged to your grandfather Saul, and you will always eat at my table." **Mephibosheth bowed down and said, "What is your servant, that you should notice a dead dog like me?"** Then the king summoned Ziba, Saul's servant, and said to him, "I have given your master's grandson everything that belonged to Saul and his family."
>
> –II Samuel 9:6-9 (Emphasis mine)

Whether the wounded one is able to "make it happen" or not, if they're in our reach and they're lacking something, we must be concerned enough to see to it that they are restored.

Point three: Taking on the burden of restoration pleases Christ!

> Carry each other's burdens, and in this way you will fulfill the law of Christ.
>
> –Galatians 6:2

While the temptation is simply to concern yourself with your own progress, the body of Christ is where His real concern lies. It is significant for us to demonstrate "body concern." This is one of the great messages Christ came to share.

Here's the deal. We really have no other choice. No matter how we've been affected, how we have failed, or what we've done, because of the wonderful tool God has given us in restoration, we are overcomers! The task now is getting others to see it, accept it, and live it. I'm more encouraged than ever that you who are reading this book will experience progress like you've never seen. You've probably experienced things that have killed others. You have survived because there's still more for you to do. Maybe you've tripped over something. Maybe you have tripped more than once. Here is the wonderful message that I have received to give to you. No matter what you have tripped over or experienced, remember: *Failure Ain't Final!*

THE BEGINING

No one else can create your new beginning. They can only create the perfect environment for it to take place!

–Brian Anderson-Payne

ABOUT THE AUTHOR

Pastor, author, recording artist, entrepreneur, speaker, Brian Anderson-Payne was placed in a chair to preach his first sermon before age 10. More than 25 years later, many find comfort, guidance and answers in the sermons reached by this psychological type preacher.

"Don't complain about a world YOU won't attempt to change!" That's his code, his quote & his compass!

As a songwriter, BAP has recorded with Rodnie Bryant & the Christian Community Mass Choir, The Brian Anderson-Payne Project, Gospel meets the Indianapolis Symphony Orchestra, Edwin Hawkins Love Fellowship Seminar, The Georgia Mass Choir, JDI Records, The Gospel Music Workshop of America Youth Choir and others.

CEO of BAP Ministries, Inc, (BAPM). BAPM is the umbrella organization for the Body of Christ Family Reunion; Out Tha' Box, Hagar's Heart Single Mothers Program & A Shepherds Song (Musical concert featuring senior pastors).

In 2008 The BAP Project Publishing Company recorded Brian's first full length Gospel CD, *'The Music of the Message'*. One of the first of its kind, the CD was accompanied by a companion book of the same title.

As a public speaker, Brian travels extensively with his down-to-earth, scripturally strong message that God loves *everyone* period!